THE CHURCH

The Church Down Our Street

A Guide to Everyday Evangelism

MICHAEL WOODERSON

MARC

Eastbourne

Biblical quotations are from the
Good News Bible © American Bible Society 1976
Published by the Bible Societies and Collins

Front cover photos by Mick Rock and Nigel Blythe,
Cephas Picture Library

British Library Cataloguing in Publication Data

Wooderson, Michael
The church down our street.
1. Christian church. Parish work.
Evangelism
I. Title
253.7

ISBN 1-85424-031-5

Production and printing in Great Britain for
MARC, an imprint of Monarch Publications
1 St Anne's Road, Eastbourne, E Sussex BN21 3UN
by Nuprint Ltd, Harpenden, Herts AL5 4SE.

Acknowledgements

I should like to thank Tony Collins for persuading me to attempt the book, and those who, without always knowing it, nudged me to keep writing when I wondered whether it really was time well spent.

I owe a special debt to Ginny for her encouragement and her perceptive comments when the book was in its early stages and for spending Christmas reading the first draft and suggesting modifications.

I am also grateful to Sue for letting me try it out on her. Mary, Hazel and Jill all helped with the typing at various stages and I express my thanks to them.

Above all I wish to thank those people who have allowed me to tell their stories without which these pages would be very dull.

Dedication

For Ann,
wife, lover, friend, critic,
and fellow-minister of the gospel;
and for Michelle and Mark,
who let me scribble away when I
should have been with them.

CONTENTS

FOREWORD
BY
REVD DR ROY POINTER

THIS IS A BOOK that many have been waiting for. It is the thrilling story of how God works through the witness of his very ordinary people to bring others to faith in him. It describes the development and use of a programme of evangelism by Michael Wooderson in two Anglican parishes. This evangelism programme is better known by the title 'Good News Down the Street' and has been used in many different churches with remarkable effect.

This book will increase your faith in the power of the Gospel, and your confidence in its relevance for today. Far too many church leaders continue to bemoan the hard-heartedness of contemporary Britons, and imply that our nation cannot be reached by the gospel. Michael's experience challenges this unbelief and calls us to the task of winning our peoples for Christ. As you read the many stories of lives changed by the power of the Holy Spirit, I pray that you will feel compelled to obey the Great Commission and go and make disciples, too.

The great strengths of Michael's story are that the lessons learned by him and passed to us are easy to learn and apply. His enthusiasm is contagious, and his experience can be copied. Your church can do what his has done!

The programme is simple and practical in its approach. Biblical principles for evangelism have been worked out in practical activities that are well within the resources of the ordinary and even smallest local church.

The stress on lay involvement and their mobilisation in evangelism is the key to the programme's success. And the ability to relate the witness of ordinary church members to those 'windows of receptivity' of the unchurched, when they come to church for the 'rites of passage' and for Christian festivals, is a lesson for us all.

The book has much to offer discerning ministers who are eager to do the work of an evangelist, and to equip their church members to share the good news. But like Michael they must be willing to face the risk of releasing the laity.

Notice, as you read, the way the gospel spreads through networks of relationships and travels from one group of people to another. Recognise the importance of the family and friends of new converts being brought to faith in Christ by the witness of someone they know and love. And follow the progress of prayer!

This story reads like the Gospels and the Acts of the Apostles all over again with Dave, John and Christine, modern-day counterparts of Gaius, Aquila and Priscilla.

There is much to learn, too, about the care of new Christians and their incorporation into the life of the local church. Be sure to note the remarkable way in which they can become witnesses for Christ so soon after conversion.

Michael has much to teach all who want to engage in effective evangelism today. I warmly commend his book to all who are concerned to see that the good news of Jesus Christ is heard down their street.

Revd Dr Roy Pointer
Director for Church Training
Bible Society

PREFACE

IN THESE PAGES I have tried to set down without exaggeration the story of what God has done and is continuing to do in two ordinary Anglican parishes. I am aware that in the very act of setting down their story I may have made them appear less ordinary than they are. If that is so, I will have done them and you a disservice. The people and the parishes *are* ordinary. They have the same faults and failings, ups and downs, successes and failures, as do any other Christian communities.

In telling the story I have had to select and arrange the material to convey as clearly as possible the impact God has made on people's lives in one area of the church's life—its evangelistic activity—and even that only in relation to one particular scheme of outreach. While the teams have been the catalyst for action in those parishes, and a medium that God has greatly used, he has of course been breaking into people's lives in other ways that I have not chronicled.

My prayer and longing is that many more churches will be encouraged to experiment boldly with this and other ways of sharing the good news of the kingdom of God. It is only when the ordinary Christians in the local community are released to share their faith that the Church starts to become credible in the eyes of the world.

The people whose story I have tried to tell are no different from people in any other part of the country. They had the same misgivings about embarking on such an enterprise as would any ordinary church members anywhere. In their inexperience they have not always handled situations in the best text-book manner, I am sure. But what has shone through is their genuineness. By the grace of God they have not been put off by hard questions, disruptive children, intrusive television programmes, the disappointment of failure, nor by any of the wiles of the Enemy. They have drawn strength from the Lord and from one another and have pressed on regardless. The example of their whole-hearted commitment to God, their honest humanity, their willingness to face up to the difficulties posed by believing (without recourse to glib clichés or slick quotes from Scripture—few of them know enough to be capable of hiding in that way!); all these have done more than anything to convince people that Jesus Christ is indeed good news. When the Spirit of God sets to work on ordinary lives their very ordinariness reveals the power of our extraordinary God.

Long may it be so!

CHAPTER ONE

LIFE NORTH OF WATFORD

JUNE IS A GOOD TIME to move into a new parish, unless you suffer with hay fever and are moving from the south to the north! The season that summer of 1973 seemed interminable. I most definitely did not appreciate the hot, dry spell that welcomed us on our arrival in the Midlands. I spent most of the first six weeks in Aldridge sneezing my way from place to place, hiding behind dark glasses, removing them only when I had to, keeping indoors as much as possible. I would have liked to take the Sunday services in sunglasses but could not quite bring myself to do so. As for the flowers so lovingly arranged on a pedestal beside my stall in the sanctuary, they were a source of torment to my already sensitive nostrils. I cannot think those early services were very memorable.

Culture shock

Nevertheless, June is a good time to move. Most parishes, except those in tourist areas, begin to wind down as people come and go on their holidays. I had three months to find my feet before the normal round of activities of parish life began in September. Ann and I revelled in the more leisurely pace of life in general. What a contrast to London, where everyone lived such hectic lives! Here we noticed that people had time to stop and chat. Shops weren't just places that sold goods; they were meeting points for the community. Shopkeepers weren't just there to take your money and pass on to the next customer as swiftly and efficiently as possible; they were known by and knew personally many of the people whom they served. They were receivers and dispensers of local information. It was in the Lazy Hill Post Office that we discovered that Mary Smith had given birth to her third; and the day, the time, the weight and the colour of the eyes were issued along with the Family Allowance, the stamps and the postal orders. It was in the grocer's that we were given the latest bulletin on old Fred's progress since his fall last week. I, in particular, had to adjust to not just rushing into a shop and rushing out again with my purchase. It was not a virtue to be always in a hurry. My years in Africa ought to have taught me that.

We had also to get to grips with the unfamiliar turns of phrase and strange grammatical constructions in a variety of Midlands and Black Country accents. An 'outdoor' had us completely baffled. 'It's next to the outdoor' was the helpful reply to my enquiry about the electrical shop. 'Thanks,' I said with a smile, not daring to enquire further for fear of showing my ignorance.

'What on earth is an outdoor?' I exclaimed to Ann when I returned to the car. 'Do you think it's an outside loo?' she suggested with her usual intuitive brilliance.

'It can't be that,' I said, 'the electrical shop's supposed to be next to it.'

'Then perhaps it's a public loo', she persisted. 'Why didn't you ask?'

'I haven't seen a public loo anywhere around here,' I said, avoiding the question. 'Anyway, the shop will be shut by now. Let's go home and I'll ask Eric when I see him tonight.'

Eric, one of the churchwardens, fell about laughing at our speculative definition of an 'outdoor'. No wonder! The mysterious 'outdoor' was none other than an off-licence. But how could an 'incomer' be expected to know that?

My next encounter with the language barrier was more disturbing. Still feeling rather conscious of being a stranger in these parts, I was concerned to overhear the remark, 'Lots of people do foreigners around here.' *Perhaps the natives aren't as friendly as they seem*! I thought. *They may not even like southerners*. I was relieved to discover that 'doing a foreigner' was nothing more violent than doing a job for someone 'on the side', as we would have said down south.

Little by little we absorbed the vernacular, and by dint of hard listening could soon grasp most of what was being said to us without the need for an interpreter!

There were surprises for us also in the religious sphere, in two areas—the attitudes of the clergy, and the degree of residual Christianity among the people. Coming from the Southwark Diocese with its considerable quota of unconventional clergy, where Post-Ordination Training was a colourful affair, and there was a marked absence of traditional clerical attire, to the Lichfield Diocese, where all the clergy seemed to wear their clerical collars all the time, and observe all the formalities—was like taking a journey back in time. It all seemed very old-fashioned and unnecessarily stuffy. Clericalism ruled—and it was not OK! Much has changed for the better since I suffered that culture shock in 1973.

The other surprise was the extent of what has been called 'folk religion', particularly surrounding birth and death. In suburban London it seemed to be practically extinct. I remember only one request for 'churching' during my four years as a curate at St Lawrence's, Morden. But in Aldridge there was a steady trickle, in almost every case because Granny wouldn't let the parents in the house until the baby had been taken into church. Memorial services, when the family and friends of the deceased attend church on the Sunday after the funeral, were then unheard of in the south; here they were the norm. On a winter's evening it is nothing to have a church full of mourners, outnumbering the regular congregation by three to one.

St Thomas'

The process of adjustment was greatly aided by my being part of a parish team. I had been used to working in a team in Morden, albeit as the junior member on a staff of six responsible for four churches. In Aldridge the team was

somewhat smaller. As curate-in-charge of St Thomas', on
the Coppy Hall estate, I was one of four parish staff.

John Delight, as Rector, was always a great encouragement, and it was good to have other colleagues with whom to
thrash out ideas, share joys and frustrations, and unite in
prayer and fellowship. John was keenly interested in all the
developments at St Thomas' during the eight years we were
together. I think he sometimes envied me the freedom my
situation allowed, as he laboured to bring change into a
strong but traditional evangelical Parish Church, and to deal
with all the administrative work involved in the oversight of a
large parish. But whatever his feelings, John gave me all the
freedom I wanted to develop new ideas, and I had the luxury
of a small congregation, just three years old, with no long-
established traditions, no patriarchal (or matriarchal) figures, and the minimum of administration. I was able therefore to give time and energy to developing the worship and
witness of the congregation with the minimum of hindrance.

St Thomas' was the only church building in its part of
Aldridge. Other churches were represented in the parish, of
course, but they were in the 'village' some two miles away, in
close proximity to the parish church. The Roman Catholics
had a thriving congregation on the far side of the village run
by a team of Franciscans; the Methodists enjoyed a prime
site in the main shopping area but were struggling to make
much impact. St Thomas' had the field all to itself; it could be
the Christian church for that community. There would be
people of all Christian allegiances (and none) moving into
the area. If they were to make St Thomas' their spiritual
home they would need to feel at ease in the worship, as well as
welcomed by the congregation. First impressions would be
very important.

Terry Thake, the first curate-in-charge, had wisely opted
for a pattern of weekly family services, with a service of Holy
Communion once a month preceding the family service. As
the congregation grew, an evening service was gradually
added to the pattern. It was fortunate for this community
that the era of the monolithic Book of Common Prayer had
been superceded by the era of the 'booklet'; Series Two Holy

Communion had come in 1967. Family services, following the structure of a much simplified Order for Morning Prayer, had been in print since 1968, encouraging a style of worship more accessible to the majority of the population for whom Anglican worship in its Prayer Book form was a total and utter mystery.

In structure and organisation, of course, St Thomas' was thoroughly Anglican and played its part in parish, deanery and diocese; in its espousal of a liturgy (however basic) and traditional robes it was clearly not nonconformist; yet in style, its worship was more informal, flexible and relaxed than that traditionally associated with the Church of England. In consequence, over the years it attracted and held the allegiance of many who would normally have eschewed the Church of England because of its reputation for irrelevant formality and dull, repetitive worship. The building was rather bare and functional; it did not look or feel like a 'proper' church. This was a stumbling-block for some; on the other hand it made it easier for others to come on Sunday because the surroundings were familiar to them from one of the various activities that took place there during the week. What the building lacked in beauty, mystery and awe, the congregation more than made up for in warmth, acceptance and their love of God.

Evangelism, anyone?

It was in the Spring of 1974 that the question of evangelistic outreach became the major concern of the Church Committee. A number of members expressed the need for us to find ways of reaching the many new families moving into the area, to share with them the good news of Jesus. Various suggestions were made on the spur of the moment, drawn from the experiences of one or two who had been involved in such things as open-air evangelism, a *Challenge* newspaper round, and door-to-door visiting. I expressed reservations about some of the ideas, and promised to investigate the matter more thoroughly and bring any findings back to the Committee for further discussion. I was anxious that we should not embark upon such an important enterprise without careful and prayerful consideration. My experience told me that we have to be very careful what we ask ordinary church members to do in this area, or they can be put off evangelism forever. What may work for a few extrovert enthusiasts is not necessarily best for everyone. And the one thing I was sure about in my own mind at that point was that somehow or other we had to mobilise most, if not all, of the congregation for this task.

CHAPTER TWO

LESSONS FROM AFRICA

HOW CAN WE make the good news of Jesus relevant to the people here? What is the best way to communicate the Christian faith to them? What would be likely to put people off? What could we cope with as a congregation? These were some of questions that buzzed around in my mind over the weeks as I read books about evangelism and as I visited people in their homes or ministered to them in sickness or bereavement.

An ending . . . and a beginning

The urgency of the matter was brought home to me afresh when I returned to the home of the mourners after a funeral at the local crematorium at which I had spoken about the Christian hope of resurrection to eternal life: a routine address at a routine funeral service. But something had struck home to one of the mourners, a distant relative of the deceased, and therefore more emotionally detached than the close members of the family.

As I juggled with my sandwich and my cup of tea in the crowded room, he approached me and commented favourably on the funeral service. I took this to be no more than a polite compliment to open conversation, but he then went on to talk about some of the things I had said and express a real desire to know whether they were true or just wishful thinking. The conversation could be no more than a fleeting one in the circumstances and, sadly, he had come from some distance, so our paths were unlikely to cross again. His parting words were simple: 'I would be interested in finding out more about the Christian faith.' I could only remember him in my prayers, and trust that he would take the trouble to find out more. I often wonder what became of him.

As I drove home, my mind was working furiously. I drove slowly so that I had more time to reflect on the incident. The questions jostled one another for attention. *How does a person like that, with no church connections, find out about the Christian faith?—Should I have suggested that he make contact with his local church?—But what might await him if he did?—Would he go to the library and pick out a few books at random?* He didn't seem to be the reading sort and, even if he were, I trembled to think what he might end up reading.

He might be fortunate to run across a Christian at work or in his neighbourhood and find out what he wanted to know, but humanly speaking I did not rate his chances very highly.

The more I thought about it, the more I began to realise how difficult it must be for someone like that man to get his questions answered. I had grown up in a church environment; I had always had other Christians more experienced than myself with whom to discuss the Christian faith; I had had easy access to the fount of all knowledge—the vicar! But someone like that would have to be pretty desperate before he called at the vicarage, and even if he did, the vicar would probably be out! What chance had he got?

My reflections left me vividly aware of the gulf between church culture and the vast majority of the non-churchgoing population. Seen from the outside it must look as though the churches wanted to make it as difficult as possible for anyone to discover what the Christian faith is about. It was imperative that we find a way to enable people to gain access to that knowledge without demanding from them the cultural leap required to understand church life.

Credibility gap

My mind went back to two incidents from my time in West

Africa. Engaged by the Methodist Missionary Society to teach German in French to African pupils at the Cours Secondaire Protestant in Cotonou, Dahomey (a former French colony), I shall never forget the shock of attending the first Sunday service after my arrival. I was perfectly at home in the French cultural environment and language, having spent the two previous years teaching in France; I was prepared, in theory, for the heat, the waving palm trees and the black faces as I took my place as inconspicuously as a white newcomer can.

I was not prepared, however, for what followed. We stood for the entry of the minister, an English theological lecturer from the country's Methodist Clergy Training College in Porto Novo. To my amazement, as I stood freely perspiring in an open-necked, short-sleeved shirt, he was fully robed in black cassock, gown, hood and preaching tabs! I wondered why he needed to robe at all in such heat. Was this meant to be some meritorious act, or a test of endurance?

As we sang the opening hymn I wondered, too, whether his accent would be as quaint and out of place as his dress. The hymn concluded and he launched into the introduction to the service. His delivery could not be faulted. I relaxed as the sentences flowed, but not for long. Something did not seem quite right. The words were certainly French, but the thought forms somehow sounded un-French. More than that, certain phrases seemed vaguely familiar. Did my ears deceive me? Could it really be . . .? I flicked on through the pages of the service book. There could be no doubt; the structure of the service was the same. The light dawned. Of course those phrases sounded familiar. Why, here in the steamy West African heat was the good old Book of Common Prayer duly translated word for word into French!

It seemed utterly incongruous to be standing there in 1963 as an English Methodist Minister declaimed to a French-speaking African congregation the ancient words of the beginning of Morning Prayer, 'Dearly beloved brethren . . .', knowing that next we would be kneeling to say, 'Almighty and most merciful Father, we have erred and strayed from thy ways like lost sheep', and so on through the

Order of Morning Prayer *as fixed in 1662*. I never did get used
to it. And although it was all explained to me in terms of
history and tradition (the first missionaries to plant churches
in the country were Wesleyan Methodists from Nigeria
wedded to the Prayer Book), it seemed ludicrous to me that
nearly a century later the same pattern of worship persisted,
a pattern alien to both the French and the African cultures.

What did we think we were doing? Was it some sort of
conspiracy to prevent ordinary people from worshipping God
in a relevant way? I imagined the perplexed African convert
struggling to surmount not one cultural barrier but two, in
order to join in worship in the time-honoured cadences of the
Prayer Book, albeit in a French translation. No wonder the
church only appealed to an élite and was making little
progress! This was my first real encounter with the culture
credibility gap that the Christian church can create between
itself and the community, and it left its mark on me.

Interpretation . . . ?

The second incident came in the context of an evangelistic
mission organised by the largely American-staffed Sudan
Interior Mission, which had a number of missionaries working among various language groups in the African interior.
The mission took the form of traditional crusade evangelism,
popularised by Billy Graham in the late 1950s. A large
marquee was planted in a strategic location in Cotonou, and
the usual publicity employed to draw in the crowds. The
churches in the city were involved to some degree in the
planning and execution of events, but the initiative and most
of the finance came from America, as did one of the evangelists. His name escapes me, but his methods were unforget-
table.

A larger than life Texan from the Southern Baptist Bible
Belt on an evangelistic tour of Africa, he breezed into town
with all the panache and razzamatazz of a showman. Everything he wore or carried seemed to have a Bible text on it.
Tracts were concealed about his person in every imaginable
place, to be produced 'in season and out of season', as the

Scripture enjoins. He pulled objects from his pockets like a magician and distributed them to all and sundry as if he were an entertainer at a children's party. His coup de grâce was a smart pocket handkerchief that he drew with a flourish from his jacket and displayed for all to see in bold letters a text of scripture—in King James' English, of course; what other language could the Bible possibly be written in! His audience knew not a word of English, but that did not seem to bother him. After all, he had an interpreter to do the translating.

That interpreter, trying to keep a straight face at this extraordinary performance, and wondering what on earth would happen next, was myself. As the most fluent French speaker among the English-speaking missionaries, I had been drafted into this unfamiliar role. In vain had I tried, earlier in the day, to prize from the great evangelist some indication of what theme he might be taking in his address . . . a Scripture passage? . . . or perhaps just a verse? . . . or a part of a verse? . . . a word? None was forthcoming. He was clearly a man who relied on the Lord for inspiration of the most instant variety, and on the ingenuity of his poor interpreter!

The flourish of the pocket handkerchief signalled the end of the preliminaries, and we launched into the mandatory hymn. Then, at last, the text was revealed, not, I hasten to add, on the sole of his shoes or the end of a pencil—for this was the serious business of the evening—but declaimed from a large, black King James Bible. It seemed rather an anti-climax after all the earlier excitement!

With relief, I discovered that it was a verse I knew well in French. As he read the familiar words of Isaiah 40 verse 31: 'They that wait upon the Lord shall renew their strength . . .' I mentally rehearsed the translation: 'Ceux qui se confient en l'Eternel renouvellent leur force.' I relaxed inwardly. How awful it would have been to have faltered on the first sentence! But I relaxed too soon. My relief turned to dismay as he began to give his personal testimony, full of American place-names and allusions totally lost on an unsuspecting audience of French-speaking Africans.

Worse was to come. Of all things, in his unregenerate youth, he had been a champion weight-lifter! To the amazement of my English colleagues in the audience, I did not hesitate—the value of many years reading the sports pages of newspapers, even in French! But my heart sank as I saw where he was heading—the juxtaposition of 'wait' (as in 'wait'-lifter!) and 'strength' was irresistible. He launched into an untranslatable play on words that seemed to go on forever. What I said I cannot recall. I was glad he did not understand a word of French. On he went, preaching the word, blissfully unaware that he had lost his audience completely. At this distance, I find it hard to believe that he was real. He fitted the caricature of the brash, slick, gimmicky, American evangelist so well that he was almost too good to be true.

What struck me most at the time was his total lack of any attempt to make the message relevant to either French or African culture. What he was doing, in good faith (for he was a sincere man), was so culturally alien that he might have come from Mars! So much for the timeless gospel. But was what he was doing really any worse than asking Africans with a French cultural background to worship according to the forms of the 1662 Book of Common Prayer?

In both cases the Christian faith was being presented as a by-product of Western culture and thought. Small wonder that it was making little headway, when it came dressed in thought-forms so alien to the African way of life!

From duck pond to dormitory town

How could we avoid the same pitfalls and make the good news of Jesus relevant to the people in Aldridge? I had already discovered that the people in my part of the parish came from far and wide. The Coppy Hall estate which was growing up around St Thomas' was the last of a whole series of developments which, over a period of thirty years, had transformed Aldridge from a quiet Staffordshire village with its parish church, duck pond and village green, into a dormitory town for the West Midlands conurbation.

When we arrived the estate had been under construction for five years, the church centre in use for three. It was to be a further five years before the last house was built. Not that the estate was large (800 houses); but as it was predominantly a private development, the building contractors tended to put up a few houses and then sell them before they built again. It was well designed as an estate, with property ranging from small terraced town houses, semis and bungalows to four-bedroomed detached, and incorporating a number of council properties for families and for the elderly. Many people were therefore able to move house within the estate as their family grew, an important factor in giving stability to a new community. At the geographical hub stood the church centre, a multi-purpose building providing facilities for the community (playgroup, badminton, uniformed organisations, etc) and a centre of worship.

The area of responsibility covered by the minister at St Thomas' also included two other estates, one owner-occupier (about 500 homes), the other mixed council and private (about 1,000 homes). These estates were already well-established before St Thomas' was built and therefore related much more to the parish church in the village itself. Although the church centre was central to the estate on which it was built, it was in fact off-centre in relation to the whole area it served. People living on the two older estates had no reason to come onto the new estate unless they came to play badminton or bring their children to playgroup. Because Coppy Hall was off people's normal route, many living less than a mile from St Thomas' did not know of its existence.

The majority of people in my area, on all three estates, had come from other parts of the West Midlands, many moving out from Birmingham to greener pastures; but the newer arrivals included others coming into the Midlands from other parts of the United Kingdom. There was therefore a wide cross-section of people of all ages, although young families certainly predominated on the Coppy Hall estate. Most of them were involved in industry, either on the shop-floor or in management; but there was also a good sprinkling of teachers, clerical workers and the like.

Somehow we had to find a way of presenting the good news of Jesus Christ to them in terms that they could understand and would perceive as relevant.

CHAPTER THREE

IDEAS IN THE MELTING POT

From South America

TWO BOOKS in particular greatly stimulated my thinking, although in which order I read them I can no longer recall. The first (or it may have been the second) was a book with one of the most misleading and off-putting titles you could wish for, unless you were a Pentecostal! The cover incorporated flames of fire against a black background. The whole picture simply shouted sensationalism—*Look out! the Pentecostals Are Coming.*[1] I had not heard of author Peter Wagner before; and but for the words in small letters, 'Foreword by Canon Harry Sutton', I would probably not have bothered to pick it up. Canon Harry Sutton I did know. As General Secretary of the South American Missionary Society he had preached at St Lawrence's, Morden, during my time there, and had made a lasting impression. His foreword reassured me that the book was far more serious than the title implied. I learnt that it was a book about Church Growth, and when I read:

> Mr Wagner has put into print many of the things some of us have been saying from the pulpits of the UK for several years. I have been longing for the opportunity to put in writing the substance of my preaching, but Peter Wagner has now done this for me, and has done it far better than I might have done![2]

Now I knew I could not fail to be instructed and challenged, and that in the most entertaining fashion.

I was not disappointed. Peter Wagner's analysis of the phenomenal growth of the Pentecostal churches in South America was fascinating and totally absorbing. Here was no sensationalism, but a careful appraisal of the Pentecostal movement and the factors underlying its astonishing growth. His study revealed that although the power of the Holy Spirit was the basic dynamic behind the growth, it was not the only factor. Not all Pentecostal churches were growing, but only those that exhibited the following characteristics:

They cared for the new converts in a loving community

They planted new churches as frequently as possible by a process of sub-division

They concentrated on those who were most likely to respond

They expected every member of the church to function as part of the Body

Pastors and leaders were trained on the job

Worship was joyful

Healing was used as a means of evangelism.

What an agenda! Of course, South America is rather different from South Staffordshire, and the Pentecostal Church is not the Church of England! Of course we cannot transplant things straight from one culture into another. Nevertheless there are valuable insights to be gained from the experience of churches in other parts of the world. After all, it is the same Holy Spirit who is at work in every culture. I was frankly excited by the vision of the church that came through the pages of Peter Wagner's book. For all its problems, and they were many, the Pentecostal Church in South America was vibrant with spiritual life and was making an impact on the community that the more staid and circumspect European churches do not.

My immediate concern was less all-embracing than the transformation that would be required to grow a church South American style. I registered three points of particular relevance:

Don't waste time sharing the gospel where you are not welcome but go to those who will listen (Lk 9:1–5)

Involve all the church members

Train people on the job.
These were all incorporated in the evangelistic strategy that
eventually emerged.

From Florida

The second book (or it may have been the first) was James
Kennedy's *Evangelism Explosion*.[3] This was closer to our
situation, and I read it eagerly, impressed with the simplicity
of the concept and the carefulness with which he developed a
strategy that involved all the church members in evangelism.

Working in teams of three, each leader taking two trainees,
they would systematically visit the homes in the area using a
carefully worked out and well-rehearsed presentation of the
gospel. This system had proved to be tremendously effective
and had transformed a congregation of 17 into 2,500 in ten
years. The secret was training lay people on the job to share
their faith in Jesus Christ with others in a way that gave them
confidence and therefore a desire to go on doing so.

Four things struck me about this approach:

He had hit upon a way of mobilising the whole church for
evangelism

People learnt how to share their faith by doing so, in an
environment that was not threatening

This approach actually took the gospel to people, and did
not wait until people came to church. It therefore
fulfilled the Great Commission (Mt 28:19) more
faithfully than many evangelistic enterprises which rely
on others coming to the evangelist

He had found a way of making evangelism a continuous
activity so that it became a normal part of church life,
and was not left to the few who felt particularly strongly
about it.

These four principles seemed to me fundamental to any
effective local church evangelism. I felt I had struck gold.

I was not convinced, however, that the method as it stood
could be transferred straight from Florida to Folkestone,
Fulham or Farnborough, and I was certain it was not right
for Aldridge. My misgivings were threefold.

SHOTGUN EVANGELISM

First, and most important, I was not convinced that many people in this country had sufficient grasp of what the Christian message was about to come to any meaningful decision about its relevance to their lives in one evening's discussion. In my experience very few people have more than the sketchiest knowledge about Jesus. To ask them to give their allegiance to someone about whom they knew next to nothing seemed to me to be irresponsible.

Perhaps it is different in some other countries. If people already have the pieces of the jigsaw, evangelism is to do with helping them to arrange the pieces so that they see the picture. But in the UK the evangelist has to provide people with the pieces, and that takes time. Of course there are some who do have most of the pieces, and a visit from a team is all that is needed to clinch it for them. Such are surely the exception. My own misgivings were summed up by a Baptist minister with whom I was corresponding at the time:

> A number of the suggestions that are in the air and on the market at present are too much of a shotgun approach involving almost a spiritual hold-up . . . They provide too little time to build up a relationship with the person you are talking to, and too little time for God to work in that person through the Bible.

Of course, 'Evangelism Explosion' (or 'Teach and Reach' as it is now known) has been used extensively and successfully in this country and elsewhere, and its 'clinics' provide first-class training to participants, but I must admit that my doubts still remain. It has not worked with the same long-term effectiveness in this country, and I believe that this is because we need more time than the method allows.

TRAINING, TEXTS AND TECHNIQUES

I also had misgivings about the amount of training actually required to become competent in using the method. I had in my possession a copy of the training manual prepared by the Revd David Bubbers for the congregation of Emmanuel

Church, Northwood (first used in June 1973). He had attempted to translate the method into the English scene, and the manual was extremely thorough. It was a twelve-week programme! I'm sure it was tailor-made for Northwood, with its highly educated, articulate, professional commuter population, but as I mentally cast my eye over the small, ordinary group of people that made up the congregation of St Thomas', I knew that anything demanding that amount of training was a non-starter.

Training, even when it combines theory with practice in the way David's did so cleverly, is a great barrier to a lot of people. When it involves memorising proof-texts, or mastering techniques, it is off-putting to those who found their school years painful. And training that teaches us how to deal with certain common arguments or objections to Christian belief will create more problems than it solves for people who have 'failed' the educational system. They are likely to go into a home more worried about remembering the 'right' answers than concentrating on building up a relationship of trust and acceptance with the people they are visiting. I could not see many of our people opting for—or surviving—such a course of training.

SALES TALK?

Thirdly, I had misgivings about using a 'technique', however helpful to the team of visitors it might be.

The outline presentation used by James Kennedy was clear, simple, logical and designed to produce results.

An Outline of the Presentation[4]
I The Introduction
   A The prospect's secular life
   B His church background
   C The caller's church
   D Testimony: personal or church
   E Two questions
      1 Have you come to the place in your spiritual life where you know for certain that if you were to die today you would go to Heaven?

    2 Suppose that you were to die tonight and stand before God and He were to say to you, 'Why should I let you into My Heaven?' what would you say?

II The Gospel

  A Grace

    1 Heaven is a free gift (Romans 6:23)

    2 It is not earned or deserved (Ephesians 2:8,9)

  B Man

    1 Is a sinner (Romans 3:23)

    2 Cannot save himself (Titus 3:5)

  C God

    1 Is merciful—therefore doesn't want to punish us (I John 4:8)

    2 Is just—therefore must punish sin (Psalm 89:32)

  D Christ

    1 Who He is—the infinite God–man (John 1:1)

    2 What He did—paid for our sins and purchased a place in Heaven for us (Isaiah 53:4) which He offers as a gift that may be received by . . .

  E Faith

    1 What it is not—mere intellectual assent nor temporal faith (James 2:19)

    2 What it is—trusting in Jesus Christ alone for Salvation (Acts 16:31)

III The Commitment

  A The qualifying question:
    Does that make sense to you?

  B The commitment question:
    Do you want to receive the gift of eternal life?

  C The clarification of commitment:
    Would you like to transfer your trust, that is, your hope of getting into Heaven . . . from yourself and what you have been doing, to what Christ has done for you?

  D The prayer of commitment (Matthew 18:20)

  E The assurance of salvation (John 6:47)

I could see the value of this guide in giving frozen-mouthed

Christians the confidence and opportunity to share their faith with others, but I felt that the people visited were put at a great disadvantage. The initiative was all with the visiting team and did not seem to give much room for genuine dialogue on an equal footing. I know how people feel when they are confronted by Jehovah's Witnesses or Mormons, with their carefully worked out sales talk! I was also worried that an outline which is invaluable to give encouragement and effectiveness to inexperienced witnesses could become an inflexible technique which did not allow for the variety of approach needed in a genuine meeting of minds and hearts.

Nevertheless I was full of admiration for James Kennedy's work. The simplicity of the concept commended itself to me. If I did not feel happy about some aspects of it in relation to the British cultural scene and the particular parish I was in, it was up to me to devise some other way of applying the sound principles on which so much of the outline was based.

Daisies in the lawn

As my mind was occupied with these two books, the Jehovah's Witnesses made their usual visits to our estate. They appeared, like the daisies in my lawn, as soon as the better weather came after Easter. They provided another reminder of the urgency to find an effective means of reaching the area with the good news of Jesus Christ. As I watched them out of the window in my study, I reflected on the enormous number of hours they spend going from door to door with very little response, regarded as a nuisance by most people because of their persistence. Many Christians admire their zeal and dedication and feel guilty at their own timidity and lack of evangelistic enterprise. But was there anything positive we could learn from them, I wondered?

The motivation for their persistent visiting was, I knew, the need to fulfil certain minimum requirements laid down by the central organisation in America to ensure their place in the paradise on earth which, they had been taught, they would inhabit if they were good and obedient Jehovah's Witnesses. What was their strategy? The systematic visiting was aimed at discovering or stimulating interest in their views. Anyone who showed real interest would be invited to have a Bible study in their own home, which would give the Witnesses more opportunity to explain their beliefs. These studies would continue until the contact had reached the point where he or she was ready to be baptised and to become a full member of the Watchtower Society. He or she would then be expected to do his or her own quota of visits. The system does not allow for inactivity!

The more I thought about them, the more I appreciated the strengths of their strategy, even if I deplored the motivation and the false teaching which the Watchtower Society purveys. If despite the enormous sales resistance they have built up over the years they can still persuade people to let them into their homes for Bible study, how much more easily ought the Church to be able to do so! Many more people are glad to receive a visit from the church than a visit from the Jehovah's Witnesses. Surely there must be a way for us to get into homes with the good news of Jesus Christ?

All of these ideas simmered in my mind for a number of weeks without any clear pattern emerging. The break-through came unexpectedly one morning as I was shaving. I was not consciously thinking about evangelistic strategies at that time in the morning; my mind was floating freely as I went through my usual routine in the bathroom. I did not shout 'Eureka'; nor, miraculously, did I cut myself, but I suddenly knew what we had to do.

NOTES

1 Peter Wagner, *Look Out! The Pentecostals Are Coming* (Coverdale House:1974)
2 *Ibid* p9.
3 James Kennedy, *Evangelism Explosion* (Tyndale House:1970)
4 E Russell Chandler, *The Kennedy Explosion* (Coverdale House:1972), pp117–118. Adapted from *Evangelism Explosion*. Used by permission.

CHAPTER FOUR

PLANNING THE ROUTE

I<small>T WAS WITH AN AIR</small> of studied casualness that I announced the news to Ann over breakfast. We were struggling for control over a daughter of two-and-a-half who talked a great deal and ate very little, and a son of fifteen months who knew that his mouth was made for filling with food but didn't always find it first time. Between snatches of Ann's exhortation to Michelle to eat something, and attempts on my part to make sure that the Weetabix in Mark's bowl went into his mouth and not onto my lap, I explained the idea to Ann.

'What we need to do,' I said, 'is to offer people a short course of studies in the Christian faith which we could do with them comfortably in their own homes. Most of the people round here have got young families, and they can't easily get out in the evenings. It might appeal to them. We can organise teams from the congregation along the lines of "Evangelism Explosion".'

'How would you make the contacts?' Ann asked. 'Would you go knocking on doors?'

'Well,' I reflected, 'I don't think it would be much use just knocking on doors, and I don't think we've got many people who would be willing to do that. I don't know how keen I would be myself. But it would be good to work through the area gradually, street by street. If we prepared a suitable leaflet publicising the course, we could deliver it to a small number of homes and then call back a couple of days later to see whether anyone was interested. In that way people would know we were coming and that we were from the church, so there wouldn't be any danger of their mistaking us for Jehovah's Witnesses or Mormons.'

'What sort of studies will you use with them?' Ann asked, wiping Weetabix out of Mark's hair.

There I had to admit I had no clear idea. 'Perhaps there's something already on the market that we could use,' I proffered hopefully. 'I'll go across to the bookshop in Walsall this afternoon and see if I can find anything suitable.'

Any Bible studies at home?

As I climbed the stairs of 'The Beacon' to the Christian bookshop on the first floor, I did not really know precisely what I was looking for. Bible study material for non-churchgoers might not be easy to find, I thought. I was wrong. The first thing I laid my eyes on set my pulse racing. Surely here was confirmation that my 'Eureka' experience that morning had not been a purely human flash of inspiration. God was in this thinking. There on the shelf was a publication entitled 'The Way to God: A Person to Person Bible Course.'[1]

My excitement grew as I examined it. Individual work sheets with clear and simple outlines and the minimum of basic information for each of five studies, together with brief notes for the Christian worker—all contained in a small wallet; it had all the features I was instinctively looking for. The instruction sheet explaining how to use the material might have been written just for us. It set out precisely the sort of aims and methods that were buzzing in my mind:

THE WAY TO GOD
This short course had been compiled to help those who are interested in, but as yet uncommitted to, the Christian way of life.

The PURPOSE of the papers is to provide a guide for communicating the good news of the Gospel, assuming the Christian worker has a contact where regular meetings are possible and desired.

The METHOD of using the papers is essentially personal. The first part of each study sheet will contain instructions for the worker. The second part should be carefully detached and taken with you when you visit your friend.

The ADVANTAGES of this kind of course

1 The worker himself is assisted in a step-by-step presentation of the Christian good news. Each truth follows the next in content, order and challenge, so that the whole counsel of God, as far as the Gospel is concerned, is being covered.

2 The course leads quite naturally to a point of challenge or personal response. This of course should never be forced, and the individual must be left to make his own response to the Word of God.[2]

There was also a series of follow-up units that could be used with anyone who made a commitment to Christ. Although the material was designed for a one-to-one conversation, it would need very little adaptation for small groups. I obtained copies of two recommended books[3] and returned home eager to share my discoveries with Ann and begin planning a strategy to put to the church committee.

Setting out

The next meeting was scheduled for 10th June at the home of Bob and Brenda Hawkins. There were only eight people on the Committee at that point, so it was more convenient and congenial to meet in a home.

Outreach was the main item on the agenda. We held a free and wide-ranging discussion of various options before I shared with the members the vision I felt God had given me. I could tell from their attentiveness as I talked that the strategy made sense to them, and that it was something that they could see themselves and other members of the congregation involved in. In the light of this positive response, I outlined a tentative timetable for a launch in the autumn, which would give us time, I thought, to produce any literature we needed and alert the congregation to what we proposed.

Our plan was as follows:

Week beginning:

3rd September	Working in pairs, distribute leaflets advertising the course to about fifty homes.
10th September	Call back at homes to discuss whether any people are willing to take up the offer.
17th September	Further visit to arrange times and evenings for those who wish to do the course.
24th September	Study I, invitation to guest service on following Sunday.
1st October	Study II
8th October	Study III
15th October	Study IV
22nd October	Study V, invitation to guest service on following Sunday.

It was agreed that we should try to involve the whole congregation, which may have numbered fifty, in one way or another; so we decided to send a letter to everyone on the Church Electoral Roll to put them fully in the picture and to encourage them to take part.

Dear _____

For some time now the Church Committee has been concerned that we should be making a wider and greater impact upon the area as a Christian fellowship than is at present the case. It is very easy for us to get so involved with various spheres of activity, both within the Church and outside it, that we forget our responsibility as Christians to take the good news about Jesus Christ to the many people who have no connection with St Thomas' or any Christian fellowship.

This autumn we want to make a start to remedy this situation by providing a framework which will enable everyone who wishes to take part in a systematic effort to reach other people with the gospel. The scheme we have in mind is a very simple one which does not demand a vast knowledge of the Bible and the Christian faith before anyone can take part in it. All that is really required is a faith in the Lord Jesus Christ that is real, living and worth passing on.

The impact of the scheme will obviously depend on how many people are willing and able to get involved in it. We hope that you will prayerfully consider whether you can participate. Inevitably there will be some for whom this will be impossible for practical reasons, but we would like to think that everyone will be concerned to pray for this enterprise and keep informed of its progress.

Your fellow-workers in Christ,
Members of St Thomas' Committee

It was my intention to explain briefly the strategy for outreach agreed by the Committee and work through the simple studies in the 'Way to God' course, making slight modifications in the light of people's comments. To my surprise, as we went on, more and more people expressed misgivings about the study material. They felt it dwelt too much on sin and repentance and not enough on the positive aspects of the Christian faith. It was obvious that they would be uncomfortable using it. Clearly, we would have to think again.

NO THROUGH ROAD?

This was a setback I had not anticipated. Where do we go from here? I wondered. There seemed little point in pressing on to the bitter end, looking at material we would never use. The best thing to do was to cancel the remaining study meetings. We would have to prepare our own material.

'What *would* you like to see included in a course?' I asked. 'I accept what you say about this material, but what do we put in its place?'

Slowly a few ideas emerged, but not enough to build much on. I asked them to go home and think about what *they* would like to know if they were enquirers about the Christian faith. I would then try and write a course around their ideas.

I don't know whether I expected much response, but within a few days Bridget, a young housewife whose husband was not a Christian (but has become one since), called at the house with a sheet of suggestions. As I discussed them with her, I began to see the direction in which we needed to go.

The trouble she had gone to was an encouraging indication of the level of commitment to the project at the congregational level and was a real help to me as I began to design a suitable course.

By now even the revised timetable was in shreds and my new goal was to make a start before the Christmas season made everyone's lives too busy. (In the event, we sent the first teams out in the week beginning 3rd November, just in time for a pre-Christmas finish!)

Back on course

I was able to report to the committee on 14th October that the material was being revised, and that I was working on a distribution leaflet. I presented them with a complete outline of the content of the course, the details of which still had to be finalised in the later units.

It was built around two questions: 'Who was Jesus?' and 'What did Jesus do?' with a preliminary unit which was intended to set the scene for the course, and a concluding unit which sought to make a personal application of all that had been discussed during the course. There were six units in all. Each unit outline would be accompanied by a brief set of notes for the members of the team.

It was Bridget who had impressed on me the need to take nothing for granted in people's understanding of the Christian faith. I was also acutely aware of the need to produce materials that were simple and almost self-explanatory for the team members who weren't used to making a coherent presentation of the Christian faith to others. The small format presentation with as few words as possible on each sheet, so admirably thought out by the Fishers Fellowship in 'The Way to God' served as a model as I worked.

I set myself the discipline of working to an A5 sheet for each unit, both for the course outline and for the accompanying notes. The question then raised itself: 'How widely should the Bible passages range?' I did not hesitate to discount the use of Old Testament material, much as I would have liked it, because that would have meant working from the complete Bible. In the mind of the average non-churchgoer the Bible is an incomprehensible and irrelevant book with so many pages and such small print that the last thing he or she is likely to want is to read it. It is seen as good for keeping the family history in or for propping up a legless bed, but it presents a monumental barrier in people's minds.

The other problem I envisaged if we used the whole Bible was that some people—keen to show that they were not complete pagans—would want to dust off the Bible they had been given as a child and use it during the course. Invariably it would be the Authorised Version, and they would find themselves struggling with antiquated language (however beautiful in places!), and a sentence construction that would prevent rather than help their understanding. (What for instance would they make of the following from Romans 11:17–18 'And if some of the branches be broken off, and thou, being a wild olive, wert graffed in among them, and with them partakest of the root and fatness of the olive tree; Boast not against the branches.') Such a large book with its confusing arrangement of material would I was sure deter people from proceeding any further.

At the other extreme, should I restrict the course material to the Gospels, or perhaps even one Gospel? The advantage would be that people would only have a relatively small book to handle, and if we used Today's English Version (the Good News Bible) with its modern lay-out and eye-catching illustrations, they would probably be encouraged to read it. However, I was keen to draw on other parts of the New Testament which would act as a further commentary on or interpretation of the events of Jesus' life.

On balance I felt it was preferable to have the wider choice of material offered by the New Testament and was sure we could introduce it without undue problems. After all, at some point, sooner or later, people would need to read more than just a Gospel, and it might be better for them to be introduced to it gently during the course rather than have to find their way around it without any help at all at some later stage.

So it was that the course was designed to use only the

Gospels of Luke and John (in the attractive individual portions produced by the Bible Society in the Good News translation and available from Christian bookshops) for the first two units, when people were most likely to be suspicious or defensive about what was involved in the 'course' they had foolishly let themselves in for. We would use the New Testament (again the Good News paperback edition) from unit three onwards.

Obviously there would not be time to look at more than a selection of passages during the six-week course. In one sense, any selection will be arbitrary and unsatisfactory, and for those who are not used to dealing with random quotations from books, it can easily become confusing. After all, who reads books jumping from one page to another and back again?

There is, however, no way of handling so much material other than by focusing on small sections, rather as the gospel writers themselves were selective in what they included in their accounts. The drawing together of passages around a theme can illuminate the point that is being made; provided the context of each verse or passage is not abused, but is carefully explained, this can be a most helpful exercise. Although the references are sometimes only one verse of Scripture, they are not intended to be 'proof texts' but reference points for the team members, who were encouraged to provide a background and context for them. As so many people outside the church have never seen any part of the New Testament, the chosen passages provided basic information designed to stimulate interest and discussion as well as presenting people with the claims and person of Jesus Christ. I kept thinking of the man at the funeral as I prepared the material.

Another potential hazard sprang to mind. The division of the Bible into chapters and verses, convenient though it is for the initiated, is baffling for the ordinary person. How easy it would be to embarrass people unnecessarily by referring them to passages in this way! In any other book you find your place by reference to the page number. Why shouldn't we do the same for the Bible? I reasoned. There was one obvious problem—everyone would have to work from the same edition.

The only way to ensure this was to provide all the participants with copies of the Gospels or New Testaments. This would also overcome the possible complication of everyone wanting to use a different—and less easily understood—translation than the Good News. Even though providing the materials would involve considerable financial outlay, I began to see other advantages. The sight of large, well-used Bibles being handled with obvious confidence by the team would likely fill ordinary people with apprehension or make them regard the team as experts they could not easily challenge. Other Bible versions would put a distance between them and us. They would give people the wrong impression of our intentions. We wanted to encourage them to explore for themselves the truth of the claims of Jesus Christ: not to be impressed by our superior knowledge, not to feel unable to make any worthwhile contribution to the discussion. If anyone had to feel ill at ease, it would be better if it were the team members, not their hosts. So the use of personal Bibles on the course was strictly forbidden. The team would use exactly the same books as their hosts.

We wanted to encourage the maximum involvement of the hosts in each evening's discussion. We wanted them to express freely any doubts they might have; air any grievances, real or imagined, against the church, local or universal; defend opinions; in short, to unload all that cluttered their hearts and minds and was a blockage to their taking Jesus seriously.

Many people dismiss the Christian faith not because they have looked into it in depth and found it unconvincing, but because the version they have encountered has been a perversion. The Jesus whom people have rejected is not the real Jesus, but a caricature. Of course, the church, both local and universal, must be held responsible in large part for this distortion. But our task was to take people back to the sources in the Gospels, persuade them to weigh their opinions against Scripture, and pray that in the process the real Jesus would disclose himself to them.

Hence, in addition to the passages for discussion each week, each unit contained an item of simple preparation for the next session. It was not 'homework' in the generally accepted sense of the word and we always made it clear that there was no obligation to do it; certainly it wouldn't be marked! Experience has shown us that many people do continue between visits to discuss the issues raised by the team, and some people simply devour the Gospels we give them. It is not uncommon for teams to return for unit two to find that their hosts have read both Luke and John from cover to cover!

At two points in the course I felt it would be helpful to leave with people simple booklets to reinforce what had been discussed during the unit. One excellent booklet on the resurrection is entitled 'Verdict on the Empty Tomb—a lawyer looks at the facts' by Val Grieve.[4] It presents the evidence for the resurrection in a lively and interesting way, likely to hold the attention of people who may not be used to following closely reasoned arguments. The material I wished to include on the resurrection was too extensive to cover in one evening. Two units were therefore devoted to it on the original course, and this booklet was a useful bridge between the two.

We revised the course material some years later in the light of our own experience and that of others. At that time, in order to include a unit on the challenge of discipleship, it was necessary to reduce the material on the resurrection to one session. (The revised course is to be found in the second edition of 'Good News Down the Street' published by Grove Books).[5]

The other point at which a booklet seemed to commend itself was at the conclusion of the course, when people had been faced with the importance of making a personal commitment to Jesus Christ. Norman Warren's *Journey into Life*[6] was the obvious choice. Other booklets covering similar ground have appeared since, but that still takes a lot of beating. It seemed right to leave 'Journey into Life' with everyone, irrespective of their response. Any who made a clear commitment to Christ also received Norman Warren's companion booklet *The Way Ahead*.[7]

The shape of the course and most of the material was now complete. I was working on a distribution leaflet which was near completion. It was time for the next step—or so I thought!

NOTES

1 'The Way to God A Person to Person Bible Course' (Victory Tract Club:1972) for the Fishers Fellowship. Used by permission.
2 *Ibid.*
3 *Who Died. Why?* by John Eddison (Scripture Union) and *Right with God* John Blanchard (Banner of Truth).
4 Val Grieve, 'Verdict on the Empty Tomb—a lawyer looks at the facts' (Falcon:1970).
5 Grove Books, February 1983.
6 Norman Warren, *Journey into Life* (Falcon:1964).
7 Norman Warren, *The Way Ahead* (Falcon:1966).

CHAPTER FIVE

CONVINCING THE CHURCH

'**D**O YOU THINK people will really let us into their homes?'

'I'm no good at talking to people I don't know.'

'I don't know enough to be much use.'

'How will we know what to say?'

'There are lots of questions we won't be able to answer.'

'I don't think it will work.'

'Wouldn't it be better to work in pairs rather than in threes?'

'Perhaps we ought to think it through a bit more.'

The comments and questions rattled round the room as people's natural fears and misgivings surfaced. It was Sunday evening. The few Christians of long standing and experience in the congregation were gathered to look at the material I had produced and to make final preparations. Their leadership was critical to the whole project. As the discussion continued I could see the apprehension of many increasing, and resistance to the whole idea growing. Were we going to fall at the final hurdle?

'All right,' I conceded, 'I accept everything you say. After all, you are the ones who have to make it work, not me, and I don't want you to embark on anything you don't feel happy with. But we did agree that we have to do *something*, and I still think this is the way ahead. What if we set up a pilot scheme and monitor it carefully? That would give us a chance to see whether it really works. If I approached certain people on the fringe of the congregation, I'm sure I could persuade them to act as "guinea pigs".'

Heads nodded in agreement; relief spread across faces as I elaborated. People's fears were allayed. They wouldn't have to face the unknown. The ground would be prepared for them in advance. They could cope with an experiment on those terms.

Of course, it would be a little contrived, but I could see several advantages.

It would eliminate the door-to-door visits and save us valuable time. It was important to complete the course with people before the Christmas rush began, and the timetable was already tight. It was the last Sunday in October. If we didn't start within the next week or two, we would have to put the whole thing off until January, with the risk of losing all the momentum we had generated.

It would also ensure that everyone who was available to go on a team—fourteen people in all—would be able to do so immediately. No one would feel deprived, or everyone would be in the same boat—depending on your point of view. But their common experience would be invaluable.

It would mean that we could see whether having three people in a team created any problems. James Kennedy had convinced me, but the others weren't so sure. What was wrong with the scriptural pattern of going out in pairs? Surely, three Christians descending on one home would intimidate people? The test run would enable us to discover any snags and make the necessary adjustments before launching the course on an unsuspecting public.

Horses for courses

We were over the hurdle and into the final straight. But I had a lot of running to do. There was precisely one week in which to make all the arrangements.

Whom should I approach?

It obviously had to be people who were not well known to the team members, or the experiment would be worthless. We had to try out the course in a real situation, albeit one in which the team would get a more sympathetic welcome than they might expect in other circumstances. It would also make sense to go for as wide a range of people as possible, so that we could assess the suitability of the course in different situations.

I selected three young couples with children, the parents of one of our church teenagers, and a widow in her seventies, five households that had connections with St Thomas' but whose Christian commitment was either unclear or non-existent. I explained to each in turn that we were looking for different people to be 'guinea pigs' for a course about the Christian faith which we had devised and wanted to test before using more widely.

'We're not sure how well it will work and would be grateful if you could help us,' I said. 'It will involve your giving up six evenings and welcoming a team of people from the congregation into your home for a series of discussions. It's very much an experiment,' I assured them, 'so they will probably be more nervous than you.'

To my delight everyone I approached was willing to help. I stressed that I would like to visit them all after the course to get an honest and critical appraisal from them both about the subject matter and also how it was handled by the team.

My only tricky moment came at the last home I visited. Peter and Jean were a young couple who had moved into the area with their two little boys, made contact with the parish church and been referred to St Thomas' by the Rector. The less formal family services suited them better at that particular stage, and they used to appear frequently enough for me to know them quite well, but not so frequently that they were well known by the congregation. They had been involved in a church where they had lived previously, but I was not sure that they really understood what personal commitment to Jesus Christ involved. They were, however, very keen to help and wanted to know all about the proposed course. I explained that it was designed to help people who weren't Christians to understand what the Christian faith was and how it might apply to their lives, but told them we wanted to try it out first with some of the church members in order to iron out any snags.

Peter then asked helpfully, 'Do you want us to pretend that we are not Christians?' He was clearly warming to the challenge of making the exercise as authentic as possible!

I had to think fast. I couldn't tell them that the reason I had asked them was because I wasn't sure whether they were Christians or not. That would have spelt the end of a promising opportunity. Not for the only time in such situations, I heard myself using words that were not really consciously mine: 'No,' I said, 'No reflection on your acting ability, but I don't think that would work. Just be yourselves.'

Seven weeks later Peter and Jean recalled that incident with great amusement, as, beaming all over their faces, they shared with me their new-found faith in Christ. They were to be the first of many in the years to come.

Once I had secured the five homes the team would visit, it remained to select the most appropriate team for each situation. This proved more complex and time-consuming than I had anticipated. As the number of teams going out at any one time increased over the years, this part of the exercise sometimes took on nightmarish proportions; but at least for this first occasion, the fourteen volunteers were available to go out on any night of the week that suited those who had agreed to be 'guinea pigs'. We were not to enjoy that luxury again, but this time it was simply a question of matching the volunteers to the homes.

As it was important to create a good impression from the start, I was looking for points of contact between the team members and the people they were to visit. Age, background, personality, hobbies or interests, sphere of work, family circumstances—all were factors tht might provide a link between visitors and visited. If possible, I wanted there to be at least one member of the team who would have an immediate rapport with the hosts, thus helping to create a relaxed atmosphere. People need to feel at ease before they open their hearts to strangers and before relationships can develop.

Time and time again the Holy Spirit has overruled in the selection of teams. Connections, all unknown to me, have surfaced during the important first session, as people talked about themselves. People have discovered that they were born in the same hospital, or lived in the same street, or had gone to the same school—and even, on occasion, had been in the same class twenty or thirty years before, in another part of the West Midlands! They have discovered a common interest in football or fishing, music or mountaineering, cricket or cooking.

DARTS, ANYONE?

When Sue finally persuaded Nigel to allow a team to come to the house, she was most anxious that he should feel at ease from the start. On that occasion I did not do my homework very thoroughly, for I failed to discover that they were both keen darts players. Fortunately the team I selected knew one end of a dart from the other and, they told me later, spent the first half an hour of each evening enjoying a game. When Nigel made a commitment to Christ at the end of the course, they celebrated by going to his pub to play darts.

Such points of contact can be the difference between success or failure. But it isn't simply a matter of matching teams to contacts. Each team has to have the right balance within itself.

FINDING THE TRIGGER

How then should I deploy my fourteen volunteers? Everyone was willing to be on a team, but no one wanted to be a team leader! Normally confident and outgoing personalities suddenly developed unusual shyness and diffidence. Humility and self-deprecation were expressed with more than normal candour, while the next person's virtues were vigorously extolled. It was obvious that my first set of leaders would not select themselves. Our numbers were divided equally between men and women; ages ranged from late teens to early forties. There were six single people, two married couples, two husbands and two wives without their partners. This meant that the only home we were going into where

there would be a generation gap was with our sep-
tuagenarian widow, Nellie Stevens. She was a delightful and
sprightly lady, full of interest in life despite her physical
ailments, and I guessed she would get on well with the
younger set. So we sent her three of our young singles, John,
Stephanie and Heather. They felt at ease and had a wonderful time. She thoroughly enjoyed their company during those
six weeks, as became abundantly clear when I visited her
afterwards, curious to know whether she had found a team of
three a little overwhelming.

'Would it have been better if two people had come instead
of three?' I enquired. 'Did you feel outnumbered?'

'Oh no!' she said, 'I think it's wonderful that not just one
person, or even two, but *three* people were willing to give up so
much time for me. I'm really going to miss those evenings.
They have strengthened my faith no end.'

It had become clear as the course proceeded that Nellie
had a real, living faith in Jesus Christ, but, as with many of
her generation, she had never been given opportunity or
encouragement to express it openly. Religion was regarded
as a private affair not to be mentioned in public. For the first
time in her life she had told someone what Jesus meant to
her. It was a turning point; now that her faith was out in the
open her Christian life began to blossom.

My own experience as a teenager had impressed on me the
importance of openly expressing the Christian faith. I had
been a secret believer for a couple of years when my tent
leader at our church camp asked me casually as we strolled
across a field in Cornwall, 'Are you a Christian, Michael?'

I had no hesitation in affirming that I was. I had been
identified and could no longer remain hidden. By that simple
affirmation I was identifying myself openly with Jesus Christ
and from then began to grow in Christian discipleship.
Paul's words in Romans 10:9 have always seemed peculiarly
important to me: 'If you confess that Jesus is Lord and
believe that God raised him from death, you will be saved.'

For these reasons I feel most strongly that we must never
deny people the opportunity of stating where they stand in
relation to Jesus Christ. However confident we may be that

people already are Christian believers, it is important that we allow them to confess that fact for themselves. It might just be the first time they have ever openly acknowledged that allegiance, and it could be a turning point for them. It is possible to find ways of doing so without causing offence or embarrassment.

'I get the impression that you are already a Christian'—this sort of comment eases the way for a confession of faith. Afterwards it will be most natural to enquire how long they have been a Christian and whether there have been any significant spiritual moments in their pilgrimage. If we give them encouragement to tell us their story we will be doing them a favour for which they will be eternally grateful. The opportunity may well prove to be the trigger that fires them to be more open in their witness to Jesus Christ, more involved in the life of the worshipping community, more devoted to God in every part of their life.

Midwives

For the team members, however, this is often the most difficult part of the course to handle. For that reason I took a leaf out of James Kennedy's book—literally—and recommended them to use the model he sets out in *Evangelism Explosion*. I made it clear to them that it was only a model and that they did not have to use it if they had an alternative with which they felt happier. But I impressed upon them the importance of asking people to make a personal response to Jesus Christ in the light of all that they had learned during the course. This is the point at which the team leaders need most help and where they usually feel the greatest reluctance. The temptation to avoid asking for a decision—whatever it may be—can sometimes be overwhelming, and we all find innumerable 'good reasons' why it would not be appropriate in any particular case. Like the nervous young man trying to pluck up courage to 'pop the question' to the girl he wants to marry the moment of decision can be nerve-racking. 'What if she says no?', 'Will she still like me?', 'Won't it spoil a beautiful friendship?', 'Is it the right time to ask?', 'What if the words come out wrong?' However, for the sake of the people we go to, it is vitally important that they have the opportunity of declaring their position. More than once, expecting a negative reply, teams have asked people if they wished to become Christians, only to be surprised.

Brian and Margaret were a case in point. Their first contact with St Thomas' had come through the baptism of their first child, Joanne. They began attending family services once a month, and when I approached them about doing the course, they agreed. One of the team members lived two doors from us, so from time to time I enquired casually how the course was progressing. He seemed very uncertain about the outcome. Brian and Margaret didn't have a great deal to say and asked very few questions, so he found it difficult to know whether they were really interested or not. It would have been easy for the team to assume that they were not ready and to avoid putting the question of commitment to them. Fortunately they didn't; and when, rather tentatively, they asked Brian and Margaret whether they wanted to become Christians, to their surprise and delight they both said 'Yes'! Now, ten years later, they are right at the heart of the church's life and witness.

Of course the response will sometimes be 'No', as it was in two of the homes on our pilot project. I had instructed the teams carefully not to pressurise people to change their minds at this point. They must respect their integrity and graciously accept their decision. Naturally the team members will feel disappointed and may need some pastoral guidance and encouragement. But in fact such situations can be growth points in their Christian understanding. If they can be helped to see that conversion is the work of the Holy Spirit and does not depend on their human ability to persuade people, they will have learnt a valuable lesson.

Conversion takes place at the time and place of God's choosing, and if that happens not to be at the conclusion of the team's visits, they need to learn to accept that situation without being unduly discouraged or feeling that they have failed in some way. After all, they are no more than midwives assisting at the new birth. Such an understanding of their role will keep their expectations in proper perspective. In the natural course of events the moment of birth is not decided by the midwife; no more is the moment of new birth determined by our human efforts. They should indeed take heart from the knowledge that the people they have visited have had their understanding of the Christian faith enlarged, their awareness of the reality of God sharpened, their attitude towards Christians altered in a positive way. Even though their hosts have not felt able to make a commitment to Christ, the team has not wasted its time. They may well prove to have had a decisive influence in those people's lives, which will bear fruit at the right time.

So it was with Christine. She was in the early months of pregnancy when she and her husband, John, agreed to be 'guinea pigs' for one of our teams. The contact with the church had come through a coffee morning for mothers with pre-school children to which she had been brought by a friend. From there she began to attend the monthly family service with her little boy; but her husband remained aloof from any involvement with the church. If the course impressed him it would be a good indication of its value.

At its conclusion neither John nor Christine was convinced; but they had found the course of great interest, and many of the barriers in John's mind about the church had been removed. Six months later, a few weeks after the birth of her second child, Christine opened her heart to God in the quiet of her own home, and although her husband remained sceptical of her dramatic experience, she grew steadily in her Christian faith.

The late, late show?

All of this was still in the future when I met with the first three teams in the church lounge at the beginning of November 1974. It had not been possible to arrange for all five teams to go out on the same night, though three were available at once. We met half an hour before they were due at their respective homes to finalise details and to pray together. They were very nervous. One of my chief concerns was that they should not outstay their welcome, so I insisted that each team should report back to me not more than an hour and a half later. As the clock moved towards 9.30 I found myself wondering how they had got on. One by one they reported in, all within ten minutes of the deadline. All of them had been well received; that was obvious from the smiles on their faces as they shared their experiences. There was only one complaint—some of them had found it very hard to get back within the deadline. Their hosts did not want to let them go!

It was the same story when the other two teams went out later in the week. 'I can't wait for next week to come' summed up how all of them felt. It was a propitious beginning.

Each week the pattern was repeated. We met for prayer before they went out; I reminded them not to outstay their welcome; they reported back afterwards. As the weeks passed, the 9.30 deadline failed to be met by larger and larger margins. Such was the level of interest generated by the course that some of the teams could not extract themselves from the clutches of their eager hosts until well past my normal bedtime! After a couple of weeks of waiting up until 11.30 p.m. for teams to report back, I decided on a different tactic. Unless they were back before 11 p.m. I would see them some other time!

When I visited the homes afterwards and raised the question whether some of the sessions were too long, people actually apologised for keeping the teams out so late! It was not quite what I had anticipated. Of course, every situation is different and makes different demands on the teams, and fortunately for the health and strength of church members, not every team is out till midnight.

Our pilot project had been invaluable. All the participants had enjoyed the experience. The team members had grown increasingly enthusiastic as the weeks had gone by. Their 'victims' had found the experience equally rewarding. And there was the added bonus of three new Christians as a result. Our confidence was sky-high. The team members' unanimous request was 'When can we go out again?'

I knew then that the Lord had given us an effective means of mobilising the whole church for evangelism.

CHAPTER SIX

GOOD NEWS DOWN THE STREET

'WHO IN THEIR RIGHT MINDS would invite a team of three total strangers into their home for a course of studies about the Christian faith?'

Everyone asks that question, and viewed in the cold light of day, it does seem an unlikely prospect. However, fired up by the success of our pilot project, we had no doubt that the necessary contacts would be forthcoming. Nor were we to be disappointed. Even while the 'test run' was in progress, the first opening occurred.

Ray and Pauline lived barely fifty yards from the church centre; but it wasn't until they wanted their first child baptised that they had anything to do with us. When I called round to chat things through with them, it became clear that their daughter's arrival had made a big impact upon them. They were rather overwhelmed by the awesome responsibility of caring for this fragile bundle of life. There was a sense of wonder, as well as apprehension, as they talked about the change their daughter had brought into their lives. The conversation moved quite naturally from the wonder of the creation of new life into belief in God and the meaning of life.

Like many people they had had some connection with the Christian faith through Sunday School, but that had long since faded into obscurity as other 'more important' teenage activities had grabbed their attention. As casually as I could, I suggested that they might like to think through the

Christian faith again as adults. I explained that we were at this very moment trying out a new way of doing this, a way that would not involve them in the inconvenience of finding baby-sitters—because we would come to them. It would be informal and enjoyable and would not put them under any pressure. Were they interested? Yes, they were. We couldn't start for a couple of months, but that suited them. I promised to contact them again when we were ready. I left rejoicing, to break the good news to Ann. We were on our way.

Come January I had already found four homes willing to receive teams. We would not now have to canvas from door to door. The leaflets we had prepared so carefully were put away, never to be used. The other three homes all came from enquiries about baptism. It was my policy to visit each family at home to discuss the baptism service with them. I found that simply going through the order of service often threw up questions about their level of understanding of Christian things, and their desire or otherwise to know more. It gave me an opportunity to get to know them as people, to discover where and when they had had any previous contact with the Christian church, and to encourage them to pick up the threads again in their new situation. If it meant spending a whole evening with one family I regarded it as time well spent. In an area where I received between twenty and thirty baptism enquiries a year, this was a perfectly manageable pastoral strategy, and it paid dividends. Wherever anyone expressed interest in spiritual questions—and sometimes I could find myself bombarded with them (perhaps the novelty of having a clergyman captive in their lounge!)—or where there was an openness to discuss them at all I did my utmost (in the nicest possible way, of course) to persuade them to invite one of our teams to explore these matters with them more fully. It was from encounters such as these that we went into our first four homes.

Keith and Janet

If there was a low level of interest in spiritual matters, but an openness and warmth towards the church, I kept their names on a list for future visits, praying that the Lord would lead me to call on them at the right time. Keith and Janet went onto that list. They had their first child, Neil, baptised at St Thomas' in February 1975 and began to come regularly once a month to the family service. I called on them a number of times that year to see whether the time was right to suggest they invite a team. We talked a lot about football, about Keith's job, about their young child; and I drank a lot of tea and coffee. Rarely, if ever, did conversation move round to church or related matters. Keith was always the one who seemed more open to discuss such things; Janet kept the conversation to more day-to-day affairs, where she obviously felt much safer.

It was nearly two years before they were ready to take up the offer of a team. The way in for them was to be through Confirmation. I knew from the details on their baptism application form that neither of them had been confirmed. So it was that I broached the subject with them one evening, explaining that doing the preparation course did not commit them to anything in advance. It would enable them simply to find out what was involved. There would be no difficulty about baby-sitters because they could meet at home with a team from the church.

Keith readily agreed. Janet said 'No!' but was persuaded to let it happen, on the clear understanding that it was for Keith's benefit, not hers. She could sit on the sidelines and observe, if she wanted to. As she would now be the first to admit, that was a fatal mistake. It is very difficult not to get drawn in when a good discussion is going on in your lounge!

Ninety per cent of parents who bring their children for baptism have not been confirmed. They are one obvious target for outreach teams. Why not send an annual letter to parents reminding them of their undertaking to give their child a Christian upbringing and offering them a course of instruction about the Christian faith to help them carry it out? We have always had a few people take up that offer.

I have no doubt that Adult Confirmation still provides a wonderful opportunity for evangelism within the Anglican system. It has the advantage of being a traditional part of

Anglican parish life and is seen as acceptable and 'safe'. People who would not go near a Bible Study Group or an evangelistic meeting will entertain the prospect of Confirmation preparation. Most Anglican churches, because of their position in the community and their contacts through baptism, marriage and funerals, do have a fringe of church attenders who have not been confirmed.

Here are potentially active members already on the threshold of church life. Confirmation may be a once-in-a-lifetime opportunity to present the Christian faith to them in such a way that they see their need for a living relationship with God through Christ and are brought to a point of conversion. However, the traditional Confirmation class run by the vicar may not be the best vehicle to enable this to happen! Neither are Confirmation courses always designed with that end in view. Commitment to Christ can easily be assumed, and the emphasis can be on commitment to the church and all that is involved in its membership. Nor is it easy to make a personal application of the Christian message to a group of adults all at different stages of understanding. The traditional Confirmation class will also probably fail to take account of the other partner of married candidates, which means that in most cases the man of the household will remain outside the orbit of the gospel, thereby perpetuating the female/male imbalance in the churches, as well as increasing the tensions inherent in a 'divided' household.

Joan and David

I quickly saw the potential of the outreach course among those not confirmed, and it became the basis of all our adult Confirmation preparation. Rarely have I had husbands and wives both enquiring about Confirmation. In most cases the wife makes the running, while the husband happily pursues other interests, coming to church (if ever) solely in order to keep the peace. By using the teams to do the first part of the Confirmation course with people individually in their homes, there is a real chance to involve the other partner. So, when Joan approached me about being confirmed, I explained that it would involve a team coming to her home for six weeks. Would her husband mind? Or better still, would he be interested in sitting in on the course with her? She was sure he wouldn't object to a team coming to the house, but she was emphatic that he wouldn't join in!

Would she mind if I came to talk to him about it? She hesitated, then agreed somewhat doubtfully to let me try and persuade him, warning me not to expect much success. Never having met David, despite the fact that Joan had been coming to church for some time, I wondered what sort of reception I would get. I walked prayerfully up to their front door. Joan ushered me nervously into the lounge, where David was waiting. She had primed him about my visit, so he knew that I was coming to talk to him about the implications of her request for Confirmation.

I discovered that he did a tough job as a civil engineer on road construction, where he had to impose his authority on the men working under him by being tougher than they were and swearing more colourfully than they did! I was beginning to think Joan was right. When the conversation moved into the area of Joan's confirmation, I tried to gauge how David might respond to the suggestion that he should sit in on the course. It became clear that he was pleased for Joan to be confirmed, but equally clear that church was not really for him.

How could I persuade him? I put it to him that it would be nice for Joan if he sat in on the discussions. He would also know more exactly what it was she was doing and be in a better position to support her, as he clearly wanted to do. I stressed that in no way would any pressure be put upon him to get involved in the church; after all, it was Joan who wanted to be confirmed, not himself. He still looked very doubtful, but agreed to be present to meet the team and be an observer—at least for the first week.

They made such a good impression that he was present each week, getting increasingly interested in the topics under discussion. Later both he and Joan joyfully opened their lives to God and were confirmed together. The change in David was dramatic enough to be noticed by the men at work. After a few weeks without being lashed by his tongue they knew something must be wrong and tackled him about it: 'Why don't you swear at us like you used to? Are you all right?'

David hadn't noticed that he was any different until they drew his attention to it! It was simply that he hadn't felt the need to swear. He went on to be actively involved in the healing ministry at St Thomas' along with Joan.

By the simple expedient of taking the course into the homes of Confirmation candidates the way was open to involve the other partner. If they have already been confirmed themselves earlier in life and then lapsed from church attendance—the familiar passing out parade factor—it is not too difficult to persuade them to join in with their partner. They will be relaxed because the focus is not on them and therefore far more receptive to what is being discussed. It is a marvellous way of bringing to life a faith that has lain dormant for years or never more than a formality. If we are bold in taking the initiative, we shall have the joy of seeing people's faith renewed and fully Christian households established.

Alf and Joan

'Hey, Mike! Can I have a word with you?'

I stopped my bike on the church car park, surprised to get such a request from Alf. He and Joan lived in a bungalow right opposite the church centre with two delightful white Highland terriers as companions. A couple of about fifty, without children, they gave all their attention to their dogs, their garden and their home. Joan suffered from a serious heart condition and could not get about much. She found the noise of the children playing on the car park quite a strain, and Alf often had to chase them off onto the nearby field, which only made them regard him as a bit of an ogre, yelling threats at the offending youngsters and chasing them onto the nearby field. As it was the church car park, we usually got the blame for what happened on it! I wondered what had occurred to make Alf call me over.

'What's this "outreach" my wife keeps going on about?'

He went straight to the point. Joan had been coming to a coffee morning at our house with a young neighbour and had heard all about the outreach teams from others in the group who had become Christians. She had evidently been telling Alf about these unusual goings on.

I explained to him briefly what was involved and promised to come and see them both to talk about it further. When I called, not long afterwards, I was welcomed warmly but quizzed closely about the course, the teams and what was going on at the church. Their curiosity had been well and truly aroused. It was clear that they were both itching to try this outreach course, but Alf was a bit worried about his ignorance of the Bible. I quickly reassured him that the course had been designed expressly for people outside the church and didn't assume that they were familiar with the Bible at all. He wouldn't have any difficulty coping with it, I was sure. As for the Sunday school Bible he proposed fetching out of the loft, he wouldn't need to go to that trouble; we would bring all the books with us. And, by the way, we wouldn't be putting any pressure on him to go to church or anything like that. I would arrange for a team to come as soon as possible.

When, at the end of the six weeks, Alf and Joan prayed together to invite the Lord into their lives, Joan swore that the dogs joined in as well! And they were much better behaved as a result, she insisted. But it wasn't the change in the dogs that the neighbours noticed! Joan's heart condition made her prone to depression, but now she found she had new resources and a greater resilience to carry her through the rough patches. Her face expressed a peace that hadn't been there before. Although her health never really improved (she died three years later, soon after moving to Oxfordshire) she had been given a 'new life' in Christ that transformed her into an irrepressibly joyful person. The change in Alf was even more dramatic. The erstwhile 'ogre' was now frequently wreathed in smiles and couldn't do enough for people. He even seemed more tolerant of the noisy children.

What had happened to Alf and Joan helped considerably when it came to persuading the young couple next door to them to invite a team. At the very least they could see that it wasn't going to do them any harm!

The witness of transformed lives often opens new doors, if we are prepared to seize the opportunities creatively, and in ways that are culturally relevant. These are the best advertisement of all. People whose lives have been changed do not need any encouragement to tell their non-Christian friends, neighbours and relatives what has happened and how it came about. The 'outreach', as it became known, was a topic of conversation at the playgroup and the badminton club, the school gates and the senior citizens' club, at home and at work. Normal, ordinary, sensible people were vouching for the value of these 'teams' from the church. Of course, it takes a while for word to get about, but good news does travel, even if not quite as far or fast as bad.

As year follows year more referrals come from members of the congregation as they gain confidence in the scheme and are happy to recommend it to others. Once it becomes an established part of church life, people no longer think twice before talking about it to their friends.

Nevertheless, it has been our experience that the majority of openings for a team continue to come from the normal pastoral opportunities provided by births, deaths, marriages and other 'crisis points' in people's lives—crises which jolt them out of their settled routine and stimulate them to reassess their priorities, to take stock of their lives afresh, and perhaps to find new directions and new meaning. At these points the Christian message becomes a real option. If the Christian Church fails people at this point, they will be in danger of being exploited by the sects. Jehovah's Witnesses, Mormons, and worse, will certainly seize the opportunities we pass up.

However, all need not be gloom where the activities of the sects are concerned. They too can open doors for the church. Some of our most fruitful contacts have come as a result of Mormons and Jehovah's Witnesses calling on people.

Helen and John

A phone call from Pat alerted me to an urgent situation. In conversation at the gates of the Church of England Primary

School her friend, Helen, had confided to her that her husband John was very interested in the Mormons and had actually invited them to come to their home the following week to explain their beliefs. Pat felt I ought to know, since John and Helen came to the monthly family service, and their boy was in the Sunday School.

What action should I take? Should I go and warn them of the dangers of listening to the Mormons, and point out to them the erroneous doctrines they purvey? Twelve months earlier that would have been the only course open to me. But now I had an alternative that was positive and attractive—a six-week course and teams raring to go. I put it to John that as his child went to a Church of England school (of which he was also a governor), he ought at least to look thoroughly at the Christian faith before giving time to the Mormons. He agreed to cancel the visit of the Mormons and have one of our teams instead. Pat, of course, was a member of that team and had the joy of seeing Helen and John come to a living faith in Christ. Only afterwards did I discover that John thought he was inviting our team for one evening only! So much for my powers of communication. But would he have agreed if he had registered that the team was coming for six weeks? Fortunately he was too polite to protest. (We did then produce a clear information leaflet to avoid any such confusion in the future.)

Jenny and Alan

Jenny turned up at the Vicarage door one morning quite distressed. She had lived in the parish less than a year, but although she had a church background, she had not linked up with us when she moved into the area. Her next door neighbours (Jehovah's Witnesses) had been kind and helpful, however, and made her feel very welcome. The wife had soon discovered that Jenny had an interest in spiritual matters, and they had begun to study the Bible together during the day while her husband, Alan, was at work. This had been going on for some time without Alan suspecting anything untoward. He had no interest in such matters but was happy for Jenny to indulge in what he regarded as a harmless enough activity. Only when the neighbour and another lady who had joined them began to press Jenny towards baptism and spelled out their views more clearly did Jenny and Alan realise what the Watchtower Society really stood for. Alan, who only went to church once a year—on Remembrance Sunday!—insisted that she stop seeing them. The Witnesses, as is their policy, were putting pressure on Jenny to go ahead without him. What should she do?

I arranged to see her and her husband the very next evening. We spent a long time discussing what the Jehovah's Witnesses teach and why they hold their views. I supported Alan whole-heartedly in his stand, but pointed out that Jenny's interest in the Christian faith would not disappear and needed to be channelled in the right way. He was understandably anxious to ascertain that she would not be led astray again. I suggested that the most helpful thing would be for both of them to do a course about the Christian faith with one of our teams. Alan would then know more clearly what it was Jenny was getting involved in. They readily agreed. Jenny now leads one of the young people's groups at church. Alan attends church much more than once a year, but isn't yet entirely convinced.

In these two situations I rejoiced that I had a constructive alternative to offer these people who were in danger of being ensnared by the sects. How much better to be in a position to offer a positive course of action that could meet people on their own ground rather than simply to proffer negative criticism of movements whose zeal, whatever the motivation, is an indictment of our Christian inactivity!

In this chapter I have tried to give an indication of the sort of opportunities that can give rise to an opening to send in a team. The stories I have told will have served their purpose if they encourage you to be alert, bold and persistent. A fuller picture emerges from the following tables:

Opportunities for teams from St Thomas', Aldridge, to visit homes between 1975–1987 came as shown in the left columns. In 1981 I left, replaced by David Butterfield, so the second table reflects some new developments.

Table 1

	1975	1976	1977	1978	1979	1980	1981	**Total**
Baptism enquiry/ follow up	7	2	6	8	2	3	7	35
Confirmation	1	3	1	—	1	2	—	8
Coffee morning	2	7	2	—	—	1	—	12
Church notices	2	2	—	1	—	1	—	6
Contacts through wife/husband/ family	3	—	1	—	1	1	1	7
Witness of church member	1	—	—	1	—	3	5	10
Minister's visit (pastoral)	3	—	1	1	2	—	—	7
Bereavement	—	—	—	—	—	—	1	1
Over 60s Club	—	—	—	—	1	—	—	1
Door-to-door gospel distribution	—	—	—	—	—	7	18	25

Table 2

	1982	1983	1984	1985	1986	1987	1988	**Total**
Baptism enquiry	6	7	11	6	5	4	2	41
Confirmation	—	2	1	2	1	3	—	9
Through church members	2	10	6	14	8	6	2	48
Marriage preparation	—	1	—	—	—	1	—	2
Bereavement counselling	—	—	1	—	—	—	—	1
Minister's visit	1	—	—	—	—	1	—	2
Mission England	—	—	2	—	—	—	—	2
Other evangelism	—	—	—	—	4	—	—	4

These figures reveal and confirm the wide range of opportunities for evangelism within the ordinary Anglican parish simply through everyday routine pastoral contacts. The largest number of openings, 91 homes (42% of all the teams sent out) has sprung from baptism and confirmation enquiries. The fact that the Church of England is still in decline despite having the lion's share of such opportunities is a sad indictment of its lack of evangelistic vision.

CHAPTER SEVEN

OTHERS CAN MAKE IT WORK

H OW MUCH THE VISION depends upon the particular gifts of the person is a question I have been asked on many occasions. Before my move to Chasetown, it was a question I found impossible to answer with any confidence. Of course, the personality and the approach of the minister is a factor, as I pointed out in a previous chapter, and it would be foolish to ignore it. I was keenly aware that although it didn't seem enormously significant to me, that view might only be a reflection of my inability to assess properly my influence! It is very difficult to see yourself as others see you and to appreciate that what seems simple or obvious to you is only so because of your particular gifts or personality.

One couple in Aldridge to whom I led a team (without any conspicuous success, by the way) stated their conviction that the growth of St Thomas' was mostly because of my personality and approach; so that when I left, so would the congregation. I remember saying that I thought they were wrong in their observation—that actually what was happening was God's work, and he wouldn't be leaving when I did! I also challenged them to think again about the reality of God and his relevance to them when the work continued to grow after my departure, whenever that might be.

When I moved to Chasetown it was possible to test the truth of that contention in two ways. Would the scheme continue to be used under my successor at St Thomas' with the same degree of success? Would the curate at St John's be able to make it work in Chase Terrace?

Before my departure from St Thomas' I had found a member of the congregation with the right gifts willing to take on the crucial role of visiting the homes of contacts and arranging teams. This meant that there could be a measure of continuity during the transition period while my successor David Butterfield was settling in. Keith exercised that ministry for about four months and ensured a smooth transition.

Naturally enough, David himself came to Aldridge with just the same question in his mind, and with the additional question: 'Will I be able to make it work?', as he freely admitted to me.

'When I came to St Thomas' and looked at the figures of how many people had done the outreach course, my first thought was: How on earth do you persuade a couple to accept a course? Is Mike Wooderson some sort of salesman; does he sort of "nag" people, or what? My second thought was: I hope it won't take a sudden dive; I hope I manage to set up some of these teams.

'It was actually in the November, two months after my arrival, that I set up the first one—with a baptism couple; but I wonder now whether they were really ready. I think it was just me persuading them.

'The next opportunity came in the January—again with a baptism couple—and I led it myself, as I felt I needed to experience how it worked at first hand. The couple, Alan and Julie, both became Christians, and Alan is now the church treasurer. I knew then that it didn't just take a Mike Wooderson to set them up. I was convinced of my own ability, that given the right circumstances, connections, links etc it was possible to get people to do the course.'

The figures on the following table show that far from 'taking a dive' David has more than maintained the level of effectiveness of the scheme since he arrived in 1981!

Good News Down the Street: St Thomas' Church, Aldridge: 1974–1988

Year	Teams sent out	Enquirers partici- pating	Positive responses	Rededi- cations	No decisions	Not com- pleted
1974 (autumn)	5	9	3	2	4	—
1975	19	33	19	7	7	—
1976	14	26	16	3	7	—
1977	11	21	13	1	5	2
1978	10	20	12	3	5	—
1979	7	13	11	1	1	—
1980	18	32	21	1	8	2
1981 (change of minister)	36	58	42	2	9	4
1982	8	13	10	—	3	—
1983	20	31	26	—	7	—
1984	21	34	26	—	5	1
1985	21	28	15	2	8	3
1986	18	27	14	—	7	4
1987	14	22	17	—	3	4
1988 (August)	4	6	2	1	2	1
Total	**226**	**383**	**247**	**23**	**81**	**44**

In Chase Terrace, Jonathan Fox quickly proved that he was as capable as I was at finding people willing to accept a team into their home. The number of teams sent out by St John's matched those at St Anne's, and the number of people becoming Christians was similar, as the comparative figures for three years show:

St John's & St Anne's

	No of teams		No of contacts		No of new Christians	
Year	St Anne's	St John's	St Anne's	St John's	St Anne's	St John's
1982	11	10	21†	22†	15	10
1983	9	9	15	19†	13	9
1984	17	20	26†	42†	20	34
Total	**37**	**39**	**62**	**83**	**48**	**53**

† These figures include the following number of people who were already Christians:

	St Anne's	St John's
1982	3	8
1983	—	4
1984	5	1

When Jonathan and Faith departed for Liverpool in the summer of 1985 to be replaced by Colin and Jill Roome, I had a further opportunity to observe whether the success of the scheme depended on my own gifts and abilities. Colin seems to have had no greater difficulty than Jonathan in finding openings for teams, and the course continues to be used with great effectiveness in both parts of the parish.

Not only, but also . . .

Although this scheme seeks to exploit the pastoral opportunities of the Anglican parish to the full by tapping into residual 'folk religion', it is certainly not dependent upon them, as is shown by the wide use made of it in other denominations. I cite just three examples among non-Anglican situations which are known to me in more detail.

BAPTISTS

In October 1987 Queensberry Baptist Church, Nottingham, under the leadership of the Revd Cedric Parsons, launched 'Good News Down the Street' with seven teams, and followed with three more in March 1988. The church is situated in Old Basford, a downtown area of Nottingham. Dyeing and bleaching works dominated the community until the recent industrial decline. There are very few shops and no obvious focal point for the community. Rows of two-or three-bedroomed terraced houses falling straight onto the streets are the main feature of the area. The church itself used to be a preaching centre attended by an eclectic middle-class congregation who travelled in from the leafy suburbs, but the present leadership took the bold step of trying to make it a truly local church.

The measure of their success under God is that now the majority of members live within one mile of the church premises. Their minister commented:

> Contacts in a Free Church situation are more difficult to obtain, but not impossible. The church has a small visitation team that regularly calls on new people moving into the area. The sale boards easily identify the homes to visit. Four of the ten openings for teams have come in this way.
>
> One member of the church runs a secular playgroup which meets in another church's hall—there are two Anglican churches and a Methodist church in the area, none of which has its own minister at present. By her Christian witness and that of other helpers, two of whom have been introduced to the Lord Jesus and the church, a 'half-way house' has been established with the church. Three contacts came by this means.
>
> Our other contact point so far is the 'Mums and Toddlers' group run by the church members. Three of our contacts came in that way.

Any church whose members get involved in the local community and have an evangelistic vision will find the sort of opportunities that Queensberry Baptist Church is using so well. If there are few natural contacts through weddings, baptisms and funerals (the bread and butter of many Anglican churches) the church needs to take the initiative and create opportunities. A prayerful desire to be used by God, an openness to the leading of the Holy Spirit, and a warm, caring Christian fellowship into which people can be drawn—all will produce the sort of initiatives undertaken in that working-class area of Nottingham.

METHODISTS

In complete contrast Four Oaks Methodist Church, Sutton Coldfield, serves a well-established, well-appointed part of salubrious suburbia. No terraced houses here! Not a hint of a factory! The church itself stands on a prominent site and looks more like the parish church than the actual one further up the road! It is an area with a tradition of churchgoing and the attendant danger of nominal Christianity.

It boasted a good sized congregation when they began to use 'Good News Down the Street' at the end of 1984. In their situation they already had a considerable 'fringe' membership or attachment, and the scheme has proved very successful in bringing people through to a clear commitment to Christ. Two of the men who became Christians at that time with their wives are now stewards in the church and key members of the leadership team. Nearly all of the people who have received teams have done so through an existing connection with the church or through baptisms or weddings.

ASSEMBLIES OF GOD

Four years ago the Assemblies of God were led to plant a church in Norton Canes, a sprawling community of 9,000 people just to the west of Chasetown. They centred their activity in the poorer part of the community and used 'Good News Down the Street' as the main thrust of their evangelism. Starting from scratch, with no existing contacts, they worked their way from door to door, offering people the opportunity of a team. Their present letter of introduction illustrates their approach:

Olivet Pentecostal Church
Norton Canes

Hello!

I will come straight to the point. We would like the opportunity to come and talk to you. We do not want to 'bash you with a Bible' nor 'talk the legs off a perfectly good iron pot', but in a friendly, gentle way, talk with you about the life and message of Jesus Christ. Maybe you are unaware of what Jesus is doing in Norton?

We find, generally speaking, people have a very hazy understanding of Christianity, and have many unanswered questions. Someone from our church will be calling on _____ to offer you a simple discussion course for you and your family in your own home.

If you would like more information please ask them when they call or contact the above.

Yours in Christ Jesus
Pastor M J Allaway

Working in this way they gradually established a group of new converts that is now the basis of the present church. Pastor Allaway writes:

As you know, some time ago our District Council made me 'Home Missions Secretary' for the Midlands West District. This involves all areas of church planting, evangelism, church growth, etc. Our recommendation to churches is that 'Good News Down the Street' should become an integral part of the life of the church. We are also encouraging other churches outside our own fellowship (Assemblies of God) to adopt it on a regular basis.

So far at least eight churches are using it in our district alone, as well as other churches dotted around the country. We have also done presentations in other areas as well, such as the Elim Pentecostal and the House Church movement.

He then went on to list some of the ways those contacts have been made:

1 *All* visitors to church are approached and invited to receive a team.
2 All churches belong to the national 'Contact for Christ' service which refers enquirers and new converts from evangelistic events to local churches. All such referrals are encouraged to do the course.

3 Street evangelism—all contacts are invited to take the course.
4 Door-to-door leaflets (as the letter above)
5 Stress the importance of every person in the church being a contact maker. Even if they cannot always go out on a team, they can say to a friend: 'Would you like some friends of mine to come and take a course in your home?'
6 Special meetings arranged with the idea of making contacts—crusades, barbecues, barn dances, coffee mornings, youth concerts, parties, even Tupperware parties!

Clearly, the opportunities for this approach to evangelism are not limited to the Anglican parish!

Another significant figure in the tables on page 65 is, to my mind, the increasing number of openings that come through the witness of church members. It is interesting to note that during the first five years of operating the scheme the number of contacts made through baptism and Confirmation was more than double those coming through the witness of church members, even if the fifth and sixth categories in Table 1 (p 65) are added together; whereas in the subsequent six-year period the openings coming through church members match those from baptism and Confirmation. The figures bear out my contention that the scheme will be most effective if it is operated for a long time. The cumulative effect of a continuous (though not necessarily large) stream of new Christians will make its mark in the local community. The longer the course has been running in a church, the more receptive people will be to a team, as they observe the difference it has made to those who have become Christians as a result.

A similar pattern has emerged in the Parish of Chasetown to which I moved in August 1981 (see diagram opposite).

Open the gates!

Only recently a lady phoned the vicarage requesting a team. She had had no previous contact with St Anne's and was quite unknown to me. She had become friendly with Yvonne, a member of the church, whom she met each day at the school gates as they collected their children. In the course of

Analysis of Contacts at St Anne's, Chasetown
1981–1988

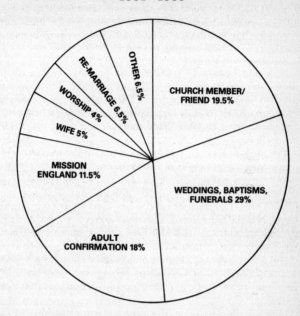

conversation she discovered that her friend went to church and expressed an interest in coming. Yvonne then told her how she had first come to join the church three years before. She told her about the team coming to her home and how much she had benefited from it. 'Why don't you ring the vicar and ask him if he would send you a team?' The suggestion had not fallen on deaf ears.

It is my conviction that there are no communities where the Spirit of God is not at work, probing and prompting, nudging and niggling, seeking to draw people to God, to awaken them to the reality of his love and their own incompleteness without him.

James Fraser, one of the great pioneer missionaries in China at the beginning of this century, wrote out of his experience among the Lisu people:

I believe that a work of God sometimes goes on behind a particular man or family, village or district before the knowledge of the truth ever reaches them. It is a silent, unsuspected work, not in mind or heart, but in the unseen realm behind these. Then, when the light of the gospel is brought, there is no difficulty, no conflict. It is, then, simply a case of 'Stand still and see the salvation of the Lord.'

This should give us confidence in praying intelligently for those who are far away from the gospel light. The longer the preparation, the deeper the work. The deeper the root, the firmer the plant when once it springs above ground. I do not believe that any deep work of God takes root without long preparation somewhere.

On the human side, evangelistic work on the mission field is like a man going about in a dark damp valley with a lighted match in his hand, seeking to ignite anything ignitable. But things are damp through and through, and will not burn, however much he tries. In other cases, God's wind and sunshine have prepared beforehand. The valley is dry in places, and when the lighted match is applied—here a shrub, there a tree, here a few sticks, there a heap of leaves take fire and give light and warmth long after the kindling match and its bearer have passed on. And this is what God wants to see, and what He will be inquired of us for: little patches of fire burning all over the world.[1]

There are places akin to the 'dark, damp valley' in our own land, places that need to be warmed and dried through the faithful, believing prayer of God's people before the gospel can be received. Those who minister in such places need special gifts of faith and prayer, patience and perseverance, as well as the understanding and support of those who work where the valley is dry and the gospel catches fire more easily. Saint Paul, as so often, put it in perspective:

Each one of us does the work which the Lord gave him to do: I sowed the seed, Apollos watered the plant, but it was God who made the plant grow. The one who sows and the one who waters really do not matter. It is God who matters, because he makes the plant grow. There is no difference between the man who sows and the man who waters; God will reward each one according to the work he has done.

(1 Corinthians 3:5–8)

The openings and opportunities may well be few and far between in some places—that I freely acknowledge—but I suspect that we also miss some of those that are presented because we are not equipped to seize them. The local community of Christians, whether it be in the 'dark, damp valleys' or the 'dry valleys' can become so preoccupied with its own internal affairs that it is unaware of what is going on in the lives of people around; or even if it is aware, it is paralysed by a sense of inadequacy and fails to present the gospel in ways that are clear and culturally relevant.

Spiritual hunger is stimulated in people's lives by the Holy Spirit; but in many places his work bears little visible fruit because the church is not prepared to offer spiritual food in a digestible form. Our experience in Aldridge was that when we as a church were ready for the task, openings for our teams began to appear. They were not at all obvious to us before. We did not think anyone would be interested. But when the commitment in prayer and the desire to be used were present, the Spirit of God went before us and brought into our orbit those who were ready to hear the good news of Jesus Christ. On the human level, having a means of sharing our faith in which we had complete confidence, made us all more alert to the spiritual needs of those among whom we lived, and gave us the courage to speak.

Spiritual warfare

I cannot emphasise too strongly the need to cover the whole operation with prayer, as Satan will undoubtedly attempt to spoil and wreck any move that people make to enter the kingdom of God. When a church first takes its evangelistic task seriously it is likely to draw the Enemy's fire. He will seek to undermine the whole enterprise by discouraging those who get involved. Team members will be vulnerable, and so will any new Christians.

John and Margaret had been Christians just three weeks when their nineteen-year-old daughter was struck down without warning by a severe cerebral haemorrhage that threatened to leave her totally disabled. They weathered the storm; their daughter has made remarkable progress and they are emerging as leaders in the church.

People who engage in evangelism are on the front line and should not expect to escape direct attack or insidious discouragement. We must press on prayerfully for the sake of those who are eager to hear the good news of Jesus Christ in the knowledge that 'the Spirit who is in you is more powerful than the spirit in those who belong to the world' (1 Jn 4:4).

NOTE

1   'The Prayer of Faith' from J O Fraser *Behind the Ranges* (Lutterworth: Cambridge, 1944), p29.

CHAPTER EIGHT

THREE IS THE KEY

'**A**FTER THIS THE LORD chose another seventy-two men [or seventy, depending on which manuscripts you follow] and sent them out two by two . . .' (Lk 10:1) Why then were we proposing to send people out in threes? What possible advantage could there be? At the time those questions were first raised I had no argument other than the purely pragmatic one: 'Let's try it and see if it works. If it doesn't, we can always revert to teams of two.'

I had to admit that both scripture and tradition seemed to point to the sense of working in pairs. There were plenty of examples in Acts: Peter and John (Acts 3:1ff; 8:14ff); Barnabas and Saul (13:22ff), then Paul and Barnabas (14:21ff)—how cleverly Luke indicates the change in relationship! Then, when Paul and Barnabas parted company because of a disagreement over Mark's suitability for the work (15:36ff), Barnabas—always the encourager—went off with Mark, while Paul formed a new team with Silas.

What I had not noticed was that on two occasions it is recorded that a third member was added to the evangelistic team. In Acts 13:4, immediately after their commissioning by the church at Antioch, Paul and Barnabas set off to evangelise the island of Cyprus. At Salamis they enlisted the young man, John Mark, as number three on the team, no doubt seeing the opportunity to train up a young, inexperienced Christian in the work of evangelism. Despite the disappointment over Mark, as soon as the opportunity arose,

Paul took on another young man, Timothy, as the third member of the team (16:1ff). Apprenticeship training has good New Testament precedent.

However, it was James Kennedy, not scripture, that alerted me to the possibilities. Fortunately the doubters were willing to try it, and our experience has proved that three is definitely best! It is the key to the long-term objective of mobilising the whole congregation for the evangelistic task, and for that reason alone it should not be abandoned lightly.

By 1981, out of a church membership of 150, 120 had been involved on teams. Of course, every situation demands a sensible and sensitive appraisal of what is pastorally desirable. It would be foolish to try and impose a team of three on a situation that was crying out for a one-to-one approach. To take but one example: Margaret was a lady of about fifty who suffered from a severely debilitating form of neuralgia that kept her in constant pain. The medication she needed to control the pain meant that there were only short periods when she was able to concentrate, and even then anything more than gentle conversation was a strain for her. A team of three, or even two, would have been more than she could have coped with. So Jean went on her own in the afternoon and was able to exercise a quiet and prayerful ministry, leading Margaret to a joyful re-affirmation of her faith.

When three is not a crowd

The more we used teams of three, the more we discovered the advantages they have. So great are they that I will never send out less than three members on a team unless the situation requires it, or unless I just haven't got anyone available to fill the third place. If the advantages had been known to me when we first launched the scheme, many of our misgivings would have been dispelled. I offer the following observations as an encouragement to any wrestling with the problem of persuading a reluctant church council, or eldership (or whatever) that it isn't such a daft idea. The order in which they are listed is entirely random.

MORE OPTIONS AND A SAFEGUARD AGAINST SCANDAL

If you follow the Luke 10 pattern of working in pairs, that severely limits the options you have for forming teams. There are only three possible combinations: two men, two women, or a husband and wife. However much church members may be trusted, it is probably not wise for a husband or wife to be out with someone else's partner, or with a single person of the opposite sex over a period of six or seven weeks. At the very least it would be open to misunderstanding, and it is best to give as little opportunity as possible to the world to criticise, to the flesh to be tempted, or to the Devil, who will readily exploit such situations.

On one occasion the third member of a team was taken ill at the last minute, just before the team's first visit. I had no time to find a replacement but did not want to delay the start. I decided to risk sending the remaining two, who were perfectly capable of handling the course. However, it did mean that a most attractive single young lady in her mid-twenties was accompanying a married man of about thirty, and I had no time to inform the couple receiving the team of what had happened. Naturally enough, they assumed that the two were married. Hurried explanations and not a little amusement followed; the ice was broken immediately. The couple expressed amazement that the team leader's wife would trust her husband to be out with such a pretty girl on his own! That time it worked out in our favour, and I acknowledged gratefully the Lord's protecting hand. But I would not recommend it as a general strategy!

The more you think about it, the more the limitations on teams of two become obvious. In many cases the course will involve going to the home of a married couple. That requires a husband and wife team. How many married couples are available for that sort of exercise in the average local church? Of those who are available, how many are suitable? What, for example, of those couples who always take different sides in a discussion and revel in attacking each other—in the nicest possible way, of course!? Their friends know that their relationship thrives on such dialogue, but it is rather confusing for strangers, and probably not all that helpful in the context of evangelism! Or, by contrast, you have those couples who always present a united front. They see everything from the same point of view; they speak with one voice, which does rather limit the range of opinions. Sometimes, one partner so dominates the conversation that the other partner might as well not be there—in which case, why send both of them?

Now there are, of course, married couples who are ideally suited for this ministry. Happy is the church that has a sufficient number of them with the time to spare to meet all the demands upon them! One area in which we are beginning to develop the ministry of married couples within this strategy of evangelism is with divorced couples enquiring about the possibility of marrying in church. Before we will make any decision about marriage in church we require them to become regular worshippers and to do the outreach course. In that situation a Christian married couple on the team is obviously an asset.

Single-sex teams can only really be used with another person or persons of the same sex, or sometimes with the elderly, who prefer a team during the day rather than in the evening. In Aldridge from 1974 to 1981 we sent out 116 teams; only 12 of those were single sex. In Chasetown from 1981 to 1987 only 11 teams out of 66 have been all of the same sex. The reason is not difficult to find. Imagine your average British male, convinced in his own mind that religion is only for women and children. He has been persuaded by his wife, against his better judgement, to be present for the first visit of the team from the church. Unfortunately there isn't a husband and wife team available, so it is two ladies who arrive, which is not surprising when you consider the female to male imbalance in most churches. He finds himself outnumbered three to one. His interest in football or fishing, darts or dogs (the racing variety), happens not to be shared by the ladies from the church, so there's not much he can talk about. He wishes he could find an excuse to slip away to the pub and vows that he won't get caught again. The end result of the visit is that his prejudice that religion is only for women has been reinforced, instead of challenged, and an opportunity has been missed. Of course, it would have been better if there had been two men available, but they are so thin on the ground in our churches that it was hardly surprising there weren't any available. But then, would an all-male team be any better from the wife's point of view?

Teams of two severely limit your options. A team of three means that you can send out the best available combination for each situation.

ANYONE CAN BE PART OF A TEAM

In a team of three there is always room for one inexperienced member.

When you begin a scheme like this one there will always be a certain percentage of the congregation who will regard it with apprehension or suspicion. Their excuse for not joining in will often be that they are not competent. Now, in a team of two you cannot easily carry a passenger, especially a reluctant one! The team leader needs a good person in support and would feel very exposed taking out a totally inexperienced person. But the number three position on the team allows any member of the church, however shy or uninstructed, to be part of a team. Invariably, when people are first approached, they express a genuine feeling of inadequacy. The conversation will go something like this:

'Margaret, you know we have these teams that go out to people who are interested in the Christian faith?'

'Yes . . .' (very apprehensively)

'Well, we have just had a request from a lady of your age who has been through a similar experience to your own, and we're looking for someone to go on the team to whom she would relate. She's quite shy, like yourself, and I think you would be able to help her. Would you be willing to go on the team?'

'But I wouldn't know what to say, and I don't really think I know enough about the Christian faith to be much use.'

'You needn't worry about that. You won't have to say anything unless you want to. I've got John leading the team, with Christine helping, and they will be able to lead the discussion in that way. I would like you to befriend this lady and just chip in with your own experience from time to time. I'm sure you would be a great help to her. Will you think about it and let me know by the weekend?'

'Yes, I will, if that's all I'm expected to do. Thank you for asking me.'

The shy person *can* just play a passive role in the group; but the informality of the home situation and the relaxed atmosphere in which the course proceeds will encourage all but the most reticent to join in the conversation and contribute to the discussion. It is because the responsibility for guiding people through the course material falls largely on the first two members of the team that it is possible for *anyone* to fill the third slot.

In 1945 the Church of England published a report on evangelism called *Towards the Conversion of England*. In the chapter on the aim of evangelism, the authors made the following statement; it is still largely true today:

> We cannot get far with evangelism until three facts are faced. First, the vast majority of English people need to be converted to Christianity. Secondly, a large number of Church people also require to be converted, in the sense of their possessing that personal knowledge of Christ which can be ours only by the dedication of the whole self, whatever the cost. Thirdly, such personal knowledge of Christ is the only satisfactory basis for testimony to others.[1]

Evangelism can therefore be a way of reaching members of the congregation whose commitment to the church may stretch back years, but whose personal commitment to Christ may be uncertain or even lacking. Such a person would be most offended at the suggestion that he needed to do the course; but he might be persuaded to join a team as number three and discover in the process that it applied as much to himself as to the people who had invited him. Rather like the Anglican clergyman, William Haslam, who, as Vicar of Baldhu in Cornwall, was converted in his own pulpit during one of his own sermons, they may discover that the message they are taking to others is relevant to their own lives. Of course, such a strategy has to be employed with great care, and the team leader needs to be carefully briefed; but I have used it successfully on several occasions.

NO NEED FOR TRAINING

'Do you *really* mean no training?'

Some people find it hard to believe that our evangelistic teams receive no training, and suspect that it is smuggled in under another name. I leave it to you to judge whether the procedure I describe below is training or not.

If I were coming to launch the scheme in your church, I would first get together as many members of the congregation as possible for an evening to explain how the teams operate, giving plenty of opportunity for questions to be raised. At the end of the evening I would ask those people who were willing to take a risk, or step out in faith (if you prefer the cliché) to sign their names and commit themselves to the course of action I had described. I would ask them to be patient until the necessary number of homes had been found.

In the meantime I would issue them with a copy of the course material and accompanying notes (as contained in the Grove Booklet: 'Good News Down the Street') and encourage them to go through it carefully, noting any things they were uncertain about. When all the homes had been found and I had arranged the teams, I would convene a meeting for the team members one week before they were due to begin. At that meeting there would be opportunity to clarify any points from the course material; I would brief them about the conduct of the evening, stressing the importance of informality and putting people at their ease; I would make it clear to them that I was available at any time if they ran into difficulties; we would pray together.

The Church Pastoral Aid Society has produced a checklist of do's and don'ts in the additional material accompanying a cassette on 'Good News Down the Street'. You may find this useful. (See page following.)

My aim would be simply to convey to them the sort of atmosphere they should try to create in the homes they were visiting.

Running the sessions— some practical do's and don't's[2]

DON'T	DO
Give them a lecture	Make it a conversation
Force them to say what you'd like to hear	Listen to what they *are* saying and make sure you've got their meaning

DON'T	DO
Pretend you have no problems	Be honest—about yourself, your relationship with God and with others, about the world . . .

DON'T	DO
Argue with each other	Pray together, plan together, work together
Get in the habit of correcting each other in front of the folk you're visiting	Encourage each other: if something needs to be said, say it later— lovingly
Complain about your church	Be positive and loyal
Talk about other people	Remember that the casual chat can be as important as the serious study

I do not believe that preparation courses which major on giving people skill in using the Scriptures or techniques for putting across the message are necessary or even helpful in the context of the sort of local church initiative I am describing. My hunch is that for many people they are counter productive, raising expectations or fears that then inhibit the natural course of conversation. What people need is not training but *encouragement* and the opportunity to gain confidence. Confidence grows when we are placed in a situation where we are welcomed, not seen as intruders; where we are accepted as fellow members of the human race and not as religious 'experts'; where people genuinely want to know about our faith because they are keen to share it. Training is intended to produce confidence, but does it always have that effect?

I suspect that sometimes the need for a training course owes as much to the fears of the minister as to the fears of church members! Ministers do not always find it easy to trust their lay people to communicate the Christian faith in terms that are acceptable to them and see a training course as a way of ensuring that the team members are 'sound', or at least 'safe', and will not misrepresent the gospel message. I have to confess that I have wondered what interpretation the teams put upon the passages of scripture that are part of the course, or how orthodox are some of the views expressed. However, it is probably as well that I have no means of knowing. I have to learn to trust the Holy Spirit to lead and guide them as they share the good news with others, and not worry whether a little heresy is unwittingly spoken here or there. God has a marvellous way of shutting people's ears at the right moment! Archbishop William Temple hit the nail right on the head when he wrote:

> It does very little harm if an eager layman talks heresy, provided he shows and imparts a love for the Lord Jesus. It does great harm if a priest talks orthodoxy so as to make men think the Gospel is dull or irrelevant.[3]

Of course, it would not be sensible to send out people who hold unorthodox views and who would be likely to use the occasion to propound them; but that is different from trying to ensure the complete orthodoxy of ordinary church members before allowing them to talk about their faith. If the gospel is to make any impact, ordinary church members need to be set free to share their faith with confidence. Training does not always achieve that end. The value of the third slot on the team is, then, that it makes it possible to involve anyone in evangelism without training him beforehand. Members learn by observing and doing, as no doubt John Mark and Timothy did in Acts.

Preparation courses, however well devised, cannot replace learning in a real situation. On a team of three, you can make mistakes and it does not matter. It can even be a positive advantage if it makes your hosts feel at ease! As people grow in confidence and experience, so they can progress to leading a team if they have the necessary qualities. Not everyone aspires to that position; many are happy to play an invaluable role as number two. However, depending on the amount of experience people are given, and their gifts and personality, it is perfectly feasible for someone to become a team leader within two years. The following list shows the sort of progress that can be made by someone starting from scratch, given the opportunities.

	Jan–Feb	Visited by team, made a commitment
	Mar–Apr	Welcome group with other new Christians
Two	May–June	No 3 in a team
Years	Sept–Dec	Further instruction
	Jan–Feb	No 2 in a team
	Mar–Dec	House fellowship group
	Jan–Feb	No 1 in a team

NEW CHRISTIANS CAN GO STRAIGHT INTO ACTION

People who are converted as a result of doing the outreach course need no additional training before going out as number three on a team. They are familiar with the material and how it works. Their enthusiasm to share their new-found faith can be channelled immediately in a constructive way. Their knowledge of the Bible may be rudimentary, their grasp of Christian doctrine elementary, but their experience of God's love and grace in Christ will be fresh and direct in its impact. A passage in Roland Allen's book *The Spontaneous Expansion of the Church* captures splendidly the power of such testimony:

> He speaks from the heart because he is too eager to be able to refrain from speaking. His subject has gripped him. He speaks of what he knows, and knows by experience. The truth which he imparts is his own truth. He knows its force. He is speaking almost as much to relieve his own mind as to convert his hearer, and yet he is as eager to convert his hearer as to relieve his own mind; for his mind can only be relieved by sharing his new truth, and his truth is not shared until another has received it. This his hearer realises. Inevitably he is moved by it. Before he has experienced the truth himself he has shared the speaker's experience.[4]

In many respects new Christians are the most valuable members of the teams. People will identify with them more closely than with the other team members. Their testimony will be: 'A couple of months ago I would have said what you have just said. I used to see things just as you do. I know how you feel. But now God . . .'

They are living evidence for the reality of God breaking into the lives of ordinary men and women. They prove what no amount of clever argument can, that the Christian faith is relevant to men and women today. They are a sign of hope to people searching for God, and they encourage people to believe that the Christian faith is within their reach, too.

'Here are people just like ourselves. If God has done this for them, he can do the same for us!'

VARIETY

It is a popular misconception that Christians are all the same. One of the fears that holds some people back from seriously considering becoming followers of Jesus is that they will lose their individuality, that their personality will be suppressed, that they will be less themselves, and have to conform to some imaginary norm. They view the Christian

life as colourless conformity, joyless morality, mindless senti-
mentality, with little room for personal expression or freedom of thought.

That view of religious people is reinforced by television
caricatures and also by the door-knocking sects whom people
will not distinguish from any other form of the Christian
faith, except that they are more of a nuisance. Their methods
and message are totally predictable, so that it does not really
matter much which pair of Witnesses or Mormons arrives on
your doorstep. They present a monolithic uniformity to the
world; they have a set series of Bible proof texts to which they
return with monotonous regularity. That peculiarity as
much as anything else is unconvincing. People instinctively
know it is not normal.

In our presentation of the Christian gospel it is important
to avoid unconvincing stereotypes. The consequence may
well be that certain members of the congregation are not
suitable to send out on teams. If you have a Leonard Thynn
among your number you will need to think more than twice
about his suitability. In Adrian Plass's delightful caricature
Leonard typifies all that is 'cranky' in evangelism:

> Leonard arrived at seven, clutching a huge brass-clasped family
> bible under his arm. Said his mother wanted him to bring it
> because *her* grandfather had used it to preach in the streets in
> 1906. Thynn was dressed in a peculiar, old-fashioned, black suit,
> that looked as if it had once been used by an undertaker. Said it
> was his *best* suit.
>
> Took up our position outside the fish-and-chip shop. Leonard
> looked like a severely deranged religious maniac out for the
> evening with his keeper.[5]

The sort of person who feels naked without a large black
Bible under his arm, or engages others in earnest tones, or
quotes scripture, chapter and verse, at the drop of a hat will
generally prove to be a severe liability in evangelism, and
cannot easily be used on a team. It is just such stereotypes we
need to avoid like the plague. Most Christians *are* normal
human beings and as different from one another as any other
group of people.

A team of three people makes it possible to bring a wider

range of views—a healthy variety—into the discussion. If my first concern is always to find a member of the congregation to whom the hosts can relate easily, my second aim is to find two others whose backgrounds, interests, jobs, family situations and Christian experience are different. Without saying a word I hope thereby to dispel the false notion that becoming a Christian reduces a person to a mindless cypher, or that Christianity is only for certain types of people, namely not my type!

So, for example, if Alan, a teacher, and Jane, a social worker, invite a team, I will endeavour to find a teacher, or a social worker, or sometimes both; then I will look for a miner or a carpenter or a bus driver, a shop assistant or factory worker or secretary to complete the team. If the opportunity arises to do the course with a whole family, mother, father and older teenage children, then a member of the youth fellowship can be an invaluable member of the team.

My attention was first drawn to the importance of such variety when I asked people in the follow-up group what they had found most helpful about the teams that had gone to them. Over a period of three years, whenever I asked that question, the answers I received always mentioned the variety among the team members.

'I was most impressed by how different they all were,' said John (who had had dealings with the Mormons). 'They didn't always agree about things; but I could see that they did have something in common—God was real and important to them.'

That comment was typical of many. I began to see that what really spoke to people was the natural humanity of the team members in all their diversity. People could relate to them. 'They were just like us' was another frequent comment. They didn't all hold the same views about everything and they could enter into lively discussion with one another while still sharing the same faith in God. Standard answers and unanimous agreement evidently were not as important as my sound evangelical upbringing had led me to believe! Of course, the team members were in agreement about the fundamental need for men and women to be in a right relationship with God, and they were agreed that Jesus was the only way in to that relationship; but, that apart, apparently they held a variety of opinions, and, praise God, it didn't seem to matter too much!

TEAMS CAN BE 'WEIGHTED'

In most situations where we gain entrance for one of our teams, the degree of interest shown by each member of the family will vary, sometimes considerably.

In many cases the first contact with the home will come through the wife, partly because there are more opportunities for women to meet and chat—the mother and toddler club, the playgroup, the coffee morning, the jumble sale, the Tupperware Party, the slimming club etc—partly because women are generally more open-minded than men and willing to consider a religious dimension to life.

'Gullible', was Robin's view; that was abundantly clear. His wife, Carol, had been coming to the coffee morning run by my wife each Wednesday in our house. She appreciated the opportunity to be with other young mothers, especially as she had a very energetic toddler on her hands. Gradually the witness of some of the Christian mothers and the discussions on various questions of faith stimulated her interest. She was keen to find out more, and a team was the obvious answer.

The big stumbling block was Robin. He would never agree, Carol was quite sure. We encouraged her to bide her time and choose the right moment to discuss it with him. (We would never go into a home against the express wishes of one partner.) I promised to come and talk to him, if that would help. Some weeks later Carol reported back disconsolately that she had got nowhere, and she wasn't very hopeful that I would either. Robin was an Oxford graduate and had some pretty firm views—one of which was that his wife was too easily taken in! I explained to him precisely what was involved in the course Carol wanted to do and reassured him that we *were* Church of England! (Not that he had any personal religious background at all.) It was clear that he himself didn't want anything to do with the course, and was not happy that his wife should either.

As he was explaining his misgivings about Carol's gullibility (as he saw it), in a moment of inspired cheek I heard myself saying, 'If you are worried about Carol being conned into something that you disapprove of, then it's up to you as her husband to be present and make sure she isn't taken in.'

Without a moment's hesitation he agreed! Perhaps he thought he would be more than a match for any team from the church.

I clearly needed to select that team with special care! Robin was the one who needed convincing, not Carol. Her interest had already taken her a long way towards finding a faith. Robin was going to make life as difficult as he could for the team. At that time I didn't realise quite how difficult he would be! I was not aware that he was an advocate of the speculations of Erich von Däniken and other God-was-an-astronaut theorists. But Robin had books on the subject I had never heard of, as I discovered when the team leader came round for a chat one day and showed me what he had lent him to read. This was evangelism in reverse. Fortunately I had two men on the team who were patient and persistent, and eventually the tide began to run in their direction.

In that situation it was vital to be able to 'weight' the team heavily in the direction of the reluctant and resistant husband.

It is important to remember that many men have never had any contact with a Christian man. They can therefore dismiss the Christian faith as irrelevant and leave it to the wife. It is still standard practice in working-class areas in the Midlands for the visiting clergyman to be directed by the husband to the religious department with the words: 'Hello vicar; you'll want the missus.'

When the opportunity arises to send a team into such a home, I want to take full advantage of it and make sure that the husband is faced with not just one but two men who by their very existence knock away one of his excuses for not taking religion seriously. The effect of that strategy is to ensure that a good percentage of men are converted and go on into the full life of the church.

Evidence of that was provided by a recent survey of the congregation in Chasetown which revealed that in the 35–50 age group, which is the one most affected by the outreach strategy we have been operating for the past five years, the breakdown is 54% women to 46% men.

A TEAM OF THREE EASES THE PROBLEM OF INTEGRATION

One of the greatest difficulties facing crusade evangelism and many other forms of evangelism is how to integrate new converts into the life of the local church. Mission England in 1984 went out of its way to tackle that problem; with what degree of success I do not know. Our experience with outreach teams encouraged us to use it even with those people who were referred to us as having made a clear commitment to Christ. It proved to be an ideal way of reinforcing the decision they had made and helping them to feel they belonged in the fellowship.

The relationships that are built during the six or seven weeks are the bridge across which people can move into the worshipping and serving life of the local church. By the end of the course, even if they have never been to church, they already feel in many respects that they belong. The fact that there are three members on a team means that in most cases they have links with three families. In a small congregation that may represent a considerable percentage!

THREE PEOPLE HELP CONTINUITY

It is important that the course proceeds without too many disruptions, lest the connections between the sessions should be lost and the cumulative impact of the material be lessened. The sessions are designed to build on one another; consequently if there is too great a gap between meetings the thread will be lost and people will not be moved forward in their thinking.

Yet it is only realistic to suppose that over a period of six or seven weeks—or double that if the person works shifts—one or other of the team members will not be available. In a team of two, when one member cannot come, it is unlikely that the course can continue. If it happens to be the team leader who is unavailable, the session has to be postponed. However, when there are three members in a team, the course can usually continue without interruption even in the absence of the leader. It is not advisable to introduce a new person into a team once the course has started as this changes the group dynamic and puts back the progress that has been made.

A GOOD GROUP DYNAMIC

In most situations a team of three members ensures a group of five, which is small enough not to require skilled leadership to make it work. It is close enough to a natural size to function without any priming. It is small enough to make sure that everyone feels involved, but large enough to prevent one-to-one conversations dominating proceedings. It gives everyone the opportunity to contribute without embarrassment, or to sit out and reflect without being conspicuous.

PEOPLE DISCOVER THE VALUE OF SMALL GROUPS

Any strategy for long-term growth will involve small group structures.[6] Yet it is notoriously difficult to involve much more than 60% of an already established congregation in house groups on a regular basis. Unless small groups are part of people's experience from the outset of their Christian lives, they tend to be seen as an option rather than as central to the church's life and witness.

In *The Liberation of the Church* David Clark makes that point. His observations certainly ring true to my own experience:

> The parish house group's major achievement has undoubtedly been in a significant move from meeting to encounter . . . it has demonstrated that it is possible for Christians to strengthen their fellowship and gain support and enlightenment in a way impossible through congregational gatherings as such. . . . Nevertheless, the parish house group has major limitations . . . local

church meetings are always assumed to take precedence over house groups, the latter being regarded as optional extras for the faithful few.[7]

If people become Christians within a small group context, having had little or no contact with the institutional church, they are much more ready to accept small groups as a normal part of Christian living than those who were brought up on a pattern of central meetings on Sunday (for worship) and midweek (for prayer and Bible Study). The small group setting of the outreach course has meant that the vast majority of our new Christians feed quite naturally into nurture groups and then into our network of house fellowship groups.

FELLOWSHIP OF CHURCH MEMBERS DEEPENS

There is nothing quite like a venture into the unknown for binding team members together, broadening their appreciation of one another and deepening their commitment to one another. Normally at least one member of the team is not well known to the others. As they pray together and support one another in the common task, so their fellowship will grow. How often do any of us spend a whole evening for six consecutive weeks in the company of even our closest friends?

We have always made it a deliberate policy to disband teams after each course, however good they may be, and constitute fresh teams for each situation. This has enabled us to give church members an opportunity to meet and get to know at some depth a wider range of their fellow Christians than would otherwise have been the case. We all tend to know a small circle of church members well and gravitate towards them. To be placed in a team with people we do not know very well helps us to appreciate better the breadth and variety of the Christian family represented within the local church. As the number of teams increases, the impact of this policy on the life of the fellowship can be considerable. It can change people's whole perception of the local church from that of a spiritual service station to that of an inter-dependent family where every member is different and all are

The Network

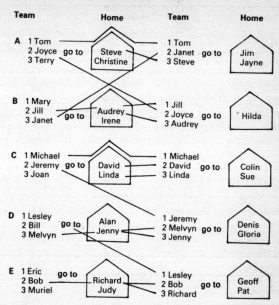

Team	Home	Team	Home

A 1 Tom / 2 Joyce go to / 3 Terry — Steve Christine — 1 Tom / 2 Janet go to / 3 Steve — Jim Jayne

B 1 Mary / 2 Jill / 3 Janet go to — Audrey Irene — 1 Jill / 2 Joyce go to / 3 Audrey — Hilda

C 1 Michael / 2 Jeremy go to / 3 Joan — David Linda — 1 Michael / 2 David go to / 3 Linda — Colin Sue

D 1 Lesley / 2 Bill go to / 3 Melvyn — Alan Jenny — 1 Jeremy / 2 Melvyn go to / 3 Jenny — Denis Gloria

E 1 Eric go to / 2 Bob / 3 Muriel — Richard Judy — 1 Lesley / 2 Bob go to / 3 Richard — Geoff Pat

important. The splitting up of teams makes a wide variety of permutations possible, as the above diagram, starting with just five teams, shows.

By deliberately mixing up the church members all sorts of barriers are broken down and new horizons are opened up.

I cannot recommend this tactic too strongly. It has brought more benefit to the life of the congregation than any other thing apart from the number of new Christians who have been added to the church. I sometimes think that it would have been worth doing simply for that benefit alone.

An analysis of the figures for St Thomas' from 1974 to 1986 reveals that during that period 204 different members of the congregation have been involved in teams, some of them, of course, many times. At St Anne's, Chasetown, in the period from 1981 to 1987 82 different people have taken part. In both churches this has had a profound effect on congregational life.

St Thomas', Aldridge

Year	Number of church members involved each year	Number of members on teams for the first time
1974	14	14
1975	53	18
1976	42	18
1977	32	15
1978	24	7
1979	14	8
1980	50	25
1981	85	18
1982	23	6
1983	51	15
1984	55	16
1985	53	22
1986	46	16
1987	35	9
1988 (Aug)	10	0
Totals	587	207

St Anne's, Chasetown

Year	Total number of church members involved	Number of members on teams for the first time
1981	3	3
1982	33	20
1983	25	9
1984	50	24
1985	15	3
1986	55	16
1987	18	7
1988 (Aug)	53	10
Totals	252	92

In the facing tables I have placed in column 1 the number of church members involved in teams during each year. Column 2 only lists people from among that number who are going out on a team for the first time. It shows how many different church members have had the opportunity to share their faith with others in this way.

Conclusion

In this chapter I have been dealing with the heart of the matter where a strategy for continuous evangelism is concerned. It is the key to releasing ordinary church members to bear witness to their faith. It is the key to ensuring a continuous flow of new Christians and integrating them into the fellowship. It is the key to renewing the spiritual vision of a congregation from the grassroots. It certainly involves a great deal of hard work for the leadership, but the rewards are also very great. It does require a whole-hearted commitment to make it work effectively, but it is within the reach of anyone who will give it that sort of priority.

NOTES

1 *Towards the Conversion of England* (London:1945), p37.
2 Available from CPAS Mission at Home, Falcon Court, 32 Fleet Street, London EC4Y 1DB.
3 *Towards the Conversion of England*, p56.
4 Roland Allen, *The Spontaneous Expansion of the Church* (Eerdmans: Grand Rapids, Michigan, 1962) p10.
5 *The Sacred Diary of Adrian Plass Aged 37¾* (Marshalls: Basingstoke, 1987) p30.
6 For further discussion on this point, see Chapter 11.
7 David Clark, *The Liberation of the Church: Role of Basic Christian Groups in a New Reformation* (National Centre for Christian Communities and Networks, 1984) p85–86.

CHAPTER NINE

STEPPING STONES INTO DISCIPLESHIP

To evangelise is so to present Christ Jesus
   in the power of the Holy Spirit
that people shall come to put their trust in Him,
to accept Him as their Saviour
and serve Him as their King
in the fellowship of the Church.[1]

THE AIM OF ANY EVANGELISM worth its salt is to produce disciples, not just converts. Considerable thought must therefore be given not only to the method and content of the evangelistic enterprise, but also to how it relates to the life of discipleship. The danger with any evangelism in the local church is to concentrate so much time and energy on setting up whatever action is proposed that the discipling of any converts is given insufficient consideration.

It is not the purpose of this chapter to rehearse ways in which this danger can be avoided, but simply to record our own experience in seeking to make adequate provision for discipleship training.

To be honest, we stumbled upon one important element almost by accident. In the days before 'nurture groups' were so called or 'caring for new Christians' was part of pre-mission training courses, we discovered the value of getting new Christians together in a small group for further instruction. It is so much easier to integrate new Christians into the life of the church if there are enough of them to form a small group than if they come in ones or twos. Now, in a large and active congregation that may not be a problem; but in a smaller church of, say, fifty or sixty members (which was more or less our situation in Aldridge when we introduced the teams) it was only possible because *we happened to start a number of teams at the same time.* At the conclusion of that initial period of outreach I had five people who needed further instruction. Fortunately, it was approaching Christmas and there was plenty going on in which they could get involved. I had a breathing space in which to work out what to do with them.

A mid-week Bible study and prayer meeting was already in existence. Could they be incorporated into that? I recognised the importance of their meeting and being met by other members of the congregation in such a group, where they could grow in their spiritual understanding and be integrated into the hub of the church's life. However, the mid-week Bible study and prayer group consisted entirely of godly men and women well versed in Scripture and accustomed to lengthy extempore prayer. They were probably studying the minor prophets or Romans or the Book of Revelation!

I could hardly drop five new Christians into that sort of study and expect them to gain much from it! Nor was it realistic to expect that small group of faithful and prayerful people to be able, at the drop of a hat, to abandon the habits of a lifetime and cease to use 'the language of Zion', the Authorised Version of the Bible and the 'thou' form in their prayers. The culture gap was too great for either group to feel at ease and understand each other on Christian territory, even though they would have plenty in common in other ways.

We decided to integrate the prayer time, but to have separate study groups. I hurriedly prepared a six-week course for the new Christians, a course which owed much to the Navigators' Bible Study materials. I arranged for the studies to be led by the second member from each of the teams which had gone to the five homes, thus giving them an opportunity to get some practice in leading a group study. I led the studies for the other group. Then we all came together for just twenty minutes of prayer, followed by coffee to round off the evening. By the end of six weeks many bridges had been built and the new Christians belonged in a much deeper way than they could have done simply by attending church services.

I was not, however, content for people simply to settle into the fellowship and become passive members, absorbing the spiritual benefits and growing fat and complacent. My hope was that by the time they had finished the mid-week studies I would have found more homes ready to receive teams so that the new Christians could go out and share their new-found faith. It never quite worked out as neatly as that. In fact, only two of the five in the initial group had the chance to go out immediately. But they did all go out on teams within twelve months of becoming Christians, some of them more than once.

As the needs of enquirers must always be paramount when deciding on the best available team, it does mean that some people get used more than others. To take an extreme and unlikely example: a middle-aged headmaster with a public school education would get less opportunities to be on a team in a new council estate for young families than would a twenty-five-year-old factory worker with two children who left school at sixteen with two CSEs! Of course the choice of team members is rarely that clear cut! The leader has to live with any tensions this may create among church members and must not be blackmailed or brow-beaten into allowing unsuitable people to go out on teams. After all, other people's eternal life may be at stake!

Inevitably, in the early years of establishing the scheme, a great deal of pressure falls on the few church members who have the gifts and abilities to lead teams. They and their families need proper and prayerful consideration. In a smaller church they will already be overcommitted, so some means has to be found to release them from other respons-ibilities if they are to lead this work, too. Any new venture like this will put pressure on existing structures and force the church to rethink priorities and methods of working.

We had to work out how to reconcile all the different demands and needs created by our venture into evangelism. We had to establish a pattern to our church life that would enable us to achieve our desired goal of being effective in our evangelism, while allowing us also to grow in spiritual maturity and discipleship without killing ourselves from overwork in the process! Reflection on our brief experience led us to certain conclusions.

Giving and receiving

Firstly, we needed a constant rhythm of giving out (through the outreach course) and taking in (through periods of study and prayer) to maintain a healthy spiritual development. As the church grew in numbers, so social action took its place alongside evangelism as another lung keeping our life fresh and healthy.

The team members found the six or seven weeks of the course spiritually demanding, for all the thrill and satisfaction of being used by God to bring others to faith in Christ. It was important that they had the opportunity to recharge their batteries; they needed to be able to draw aside and be fuelled themselves. We found that there was a renewed freshness and eagerness to learn among the church members who had been engaged on a team. Like sponges squeezed dry by the demands made upon them, they were ready to absorb afresh the revitalising presence of God mediated by the Spirit through the Scriptures and prayer. Bible study now held a greater interest because the truths learned, the insights gained, would be of value in the next evangelistic encounter as well as for personal growth. Sermons were listened to with far greater attention; there was a new sense of expectancy in the worship.

New Christians also needed this rhythm. They needed to build up their understanding of the faith they had so recently embraced. They needed to know more of this amazing God who had embraced them. But they also needed the opportunity to share what they had discovered with others. To deprive them of that opportunity would be to slow their rate of growth. There is nothing more encouraging to those new in the faith than to see God bring another person to faith through their witness.

When Michael became a Christian he went out on a team almost immediately to Keith and Janet. They became Christians in turn, and Michael and Keith went out immediately to Terry and Olwen, who also became Christians. Then Michael went with Terry to Brian and Margaret, and they became Christians too! True, that sort of chain reaction rarely occurs quite so dramatically—the opportunities are not always there—but when it does, it is an enormous encouragement for everyone involved.

The Welcome group

I have already mentioned the value of having a ready-made group of new Christians. This factor has in our estimation grown in importance since we first hit upon it accidentally.

When we had first discussed the follow-up of new converts in Aldridge, there was a suggestion that we provide material that could be used in homes as a continuation of the outreach course. It was prompted by a concern for couples who might have difficulty finding baby-sitters for the six weeks of the course. Tempting though that solution was, it was rejected because we felt it might reinforce an individualistic view of the Christian life and, in fact, make it more difficult for people to make the transition into the corporate life of the local church. The correctness of that decision has been proved consistently in the thirteen years we have used the scheme in the two parishes. The concern expressed about couples not being able to attend together has proved groundless. Such is their enthusiasm for their new-found faith that they will go to considerable lengths to find babysitters! And of course church members of all ages were often willing to volunteer.

At first we saw the value and purpose of the group simply as providing instruction in the basic elements of the Christian faith and life, taking the new Christians a little further along the way. We continued the format of A5 duplicated sheets with headings and Bible references with which they had become familiar during the outreach course. The subjects we covered were: new life, the Bible, prayer, Jesus is Lord, witnessing, the Church—pretty routine stuff. But then, we were hard-pressed meeting the clamours of church members for the chance to go out on teams and there wasn't time to devise anything original.

As the demand for teams increased, the pressure on church members meant that I could no longer use them to lead what came to be known as the Welcome group. They were needed on the front-line; I was not. There was no choice. I would have to lead that group while the established church Bible study group would have to fend for itself. It proved to be a good move. It gave me the opportunity to get close to the new Christians. It made me aware of their individual strengths and weaknesses, their personal and domestic situations, the level of their commitment, their gifts and interests; all of which was invaluable when it came later to selecting teams for outreach. It also enabled them to get to know me as a person and not just the parson, to know that they had access to the leader of the congregation at any time. Undoubtedly that helped them to integrate more quickly into church life. Of course, that is a luxury enjoyed by the minister of a small congregation; but it enables a good foundation to be laid for future growth.

While I was engaged with the Welcome group, the regular Bible study group didn't in fact have to fend for itself. My wife, Ann, offered to do a series of studies with them on the fruit of the Spirit. One significant result of that exercise was the discovery that she had real gifts in leading group discussion, gifts that would come into their own as the church grew, and as the children reached the age when they were less demanding on her time and energy.

EXPERIENCING GOD

Eventually Ann was to take over responsibility for the Welcome group and to develop it in her own distinctive way. I had tended to focus more on the content of the course, concerned that they should have some clear guidelines in the early stages of their Christian pilgrimage. She sensed that the group needed to learn the basics in a much more practical way, so that, for example, instead of just being taught *about* prayer they should actually pray; instead of being taught *about* the Bible they should learn to use it. The emphasis she brought was to make the learning experience centred, to create an atmosphere of acceptance and openness in which people were free to share at a deeper level and get a foretaste of the fellowship that is possible in small groups.

The shape of the course has evolved and now covers the following themes: assurance, prayer, the Bible, any questions?, being filled with the Holy Spirit, belonging to the Body of Christ.

Two examples will give a flavour of the sort of group experience people receive.

At the first meeting people are encouraged to share any differences they have perceived in their own lives since becoming Christians. One will be less irritable, another more joyful, yet another more thoughtful of others, and so on. Time and again, with group after group, Ann has found that the same marks of the Spirit's work emerge. She then gets the group to read together the list of the fruit of the Spirit in Paul's Letter to the Galatians chapter five and they discover that their experience tallies with Scripture. What an encouragement!

In the session on being filled with the Holy Spirit the group members are not only taught what to expect in the area of spiritual gifts and ministry, but are given the opportunity to exercise them and minister to one another. In one group Dave, a plumber by trade, was in so much pain from his back that he was forced to stand propped up against the wall. He had been under a specialist for several years with recurring back problems, and the trouble had flared up again. As Ann had finished explaining to the group about ministering to one another in prayer, and about the laying on of hands, especially where healing is involved, she became increasingly aware of Dave propped up against the wall.

His pain presented her with a predicament. How could she

just talk about the ministry of healing prayer and leave Dave as he was? But how would these new Christians react if she suggested they should minister to Dave with the laying on of hands? She need not have worried. Having explained what she felt should be done, she invited any of the group who wanted to join her to come and lay hands on Dave while she prayed. To her astonishment the whole group of fourteen gathered round. As they prayed Dave sank to the floor; hardly surprising under fourteen pairs of hands! Then, to his own amazement and the group's he got up again without any trouble. The pain had gone, and three years later it has not recurred.

The Welcome group, then, while imparting basic teaching in a number of important areas, evolved in the direction of encouraging people to expect God to be actively at work through his Spirit in their lives, in the church, and in the world.

EXPERIENCING SMALL GROUP FELLOWSHIP

The other important function of the Welcome group was that it served to introduce people to participation in the life of a small group. When we began to develop a network of house groups, the Welcome group was an invaluable transit camp for the new Christians. If people's first experience of the Christian faith and life comes through a small group meeting in their own home, and is then followed by another small group experience, they are well prepared for joining in small groups at every level.

We do need to take great care to integrate new Christians into the full, worshipping life of the church by providing a series of stepping stones for those whose background, culture or temperament, patterns of work or domestic situation create difficulties. Small, informal fellowship groups at different levels have been the most effective way we have found to look after people while they find their way into the worshipping community. Without them, I am sure, some of those who came to faith would not have gone on to become disciples.

Robin and Carol were a case in point. The difficulties encountered by the team in dealing with Robin's passion for Erich von Däniken's theories were suddenly resolved in unexpected fashion. It was a Thursday, my day off, and Ann and I were enjoying a relaxing evening together. I had my nose in a book as usual, while Ann, too, was reading. Suddenly she got up and announced: 'I've got to take this book to Robin!' The book in question was Catherine Marshall's classic *Beyond Ourselves*. I was not convinced. I couldn't see Robin even opening such a book and said so.

'With a cover like that he won't look twice at it. It looks like the front of a women's magazine! *I* know how good it is, but you wouldn't guess from the cover that it's anything other than a story for women.'

Ann sat down again. 'Perhaps you're right,' she conceded. We went back to our books. Five minutes later she interrupted: 'I've still got this feeling I'm supposed to take it to Robin.' 'Don't be daft,' I said, 'He won't read it. He'll just give it to Carol with some comment about the Christian faith only being for women.'

Again we went back to our books.

The next thing I knew, Ann was disappearing out of the door, book in hand. She had gone before I could say anything.

When Robin opened the door to her his mouth fell open in astonishment. 'Have you come from God?' he blurted out.

It wasn't exactly the sort of greeting Ann had expected, but she kept her cool. 'Yes, I have,' she said, 'And I'm a bit fed up, because I was just enjoying a good read in front of the fire!'

While Ann and I had been reading our books, Robin and Carol had been having a heated discussion about whether there really was a God and how you could possibly know. When the doorbell rang Robin had just uttered what he no doubt regarded as an unanswerable riposte: 'If God was really interested in me, he'd send a messenger.' No wonder his mouth fell open when Ann stood on the doorstep!

Two weeks later a rather apprehensive team leader asked Robin and Carol whether they felt able to make a commitment to Christ, only to hear Robin say, with a disarming smile, 'Actually, we made up our minds two weeks ago, but we didn't want to spoil it by telling you!'

However, their problems were far from over. Robin, in particular, found Sunday worship difficult. He hated singing, and with an energetic son to add to the distraction, he found the whole experience totally unrewarding. He only appeared infrequently during the following three years. Carol was more faithful, but when twin girls were added to their family, life became impossibly hectic. Except for belonging to a house group, which provided them with support and fellowship, and which for a period met in their home, they might well have been another example of converts who never went on to become disciples.

'Block' release

Another advantage of sending out a number of teams at the same time is an organisational one, but not to be despised for that reason.

It makes it easier to plan church activities without too much disruption. From the moment we launched the outreach scheme it was the unanimous decision of the church that the teams should take precedence over all else in the church programme. It was a measure of the seriousness with which people took the evangelistic task that they accepted the need to release church members from other important tasks for the duration of the course. Churchwardens and treasurers would be absent from the church council while they were out on teams; house group leaders and members would miss fellowship meetings if required.

Such disruption obviously needs to be kept within bounds and sending out as many teams as possible at the same time is a way of achieving that end. I try to give good warning when such an operation is on the horizon. This gives people time to clear their diaries, and house groups time to plan a reduced programme if they are likely to lose a good number of members. In our experience it is best not to have more than two periods of 'block release' in a year or the rest of the church's life can suffer.

Eventually a church may build up such a large pool of experienced team members that it is possible to send out teams as and when they are required. The temptation then is to operate a sort of continuous flow system, sending out teams as opportunity arises, and discontinue the 'block release' system which *can* become such an organisational nightmare (see Chapter Eight). However, although it may be necessary to send out the occasional team urgently, I would strongly advocate the value of persevering with organised periods of outreach. The more people who are involved on teams at the same time, the greater will be the impact on the congregation.

When, early in 1981, we had twenty teams operating at the same time, there was hardly any section of the congregation that did not have an interest in one situation or another. Every house group was affected by having members actively involved and was therefore prayerfully interested in the progress of the course. There was a sense of corporate involvement, of the whole church at work, rather than just a few individuals.

Block release also helps to keep outreach to the forefront of people's minds. The more widely it is talked about, the more it features quite naturally in church announcements, the prayers (without naming names, of course), newsletters and magazines, the more it will be likely to come to the attention of those who attend occasionally, and the more it will be accepted as a normal part of church life.

Marking the seasons

When planning periods of outreach activity it is a good strategy to aim to finish a few weeks before a major Christian festival so that there is a wide range of special events or services that people unused to church worship can attend and enjoy. Those who have been churchgoers all their lives do not always understand how wide is the culture gap that some people have to leap just to cross the threshold of the church even when they *have* come to faith in Christ. It is too easy to assume that once a person has taken the initial step he will move easily and naturally into Sunday worship. Christian worship, whether it be free, informal and charismatic, or formal and liturgical, or any combination of styles, is so far from many people's normal experience that it does not always have an immediate appeal. But Christmas and Easter are still reference points that people can connect with, and it is shortsighted to ignore their value. Folk religion it may be for many, but these festivals are often the only remaining link between the church and the pagan world. On these occasions people do not feel so out of their depth, especially if they can come with their children or grandchildren and be relatively inconspicuous in a large crowd. So we aim to start our periods of outreach in September or January, or both, and hope to complete the Welcome group just before Christmas and Easter. It is a pattern that I would recommend. Alternatively, Lent may be a good time to start the course, then the Welcome group can take you up to Pentecost.

Added to the Kingdom

How effectively we have managed to nurture new Christians and integrate them into the life of the church can be judged from the figures which follow. We are constantly striving to provide the right environment in which new converts can grow to maturity, in which they are challenged but encouraged to spend their lives in the service of Christ, at home, at work, in the church and in the community. Sometimes we succeed; sometimes we fail. The failures are a disappointment; but they are also a stimulus to prayer and a review of our proceedings.

In looking at the figures it is important to remember that they were only accurate at the point in time at which they were taken. They are a still frame out of a moving picture. The numbers represent real people whose circumstances, spiritual openness, level of commitment are constantly moving in one direction or another.

The figures for St Thomas' also include people who have moved out of the area, so that the 'discipleship' score does not reflect the actual number still involved in the church.

There is no means of telling whether their involvement in church life has continued in the area to which they have moved. Nevertheless, despite these limitations, the figures do provide some indication of how effective or otherwise our strategy has been. My successor, David Butterfield, and I have tried to keep accurate figures, and I am indebted to him for initiating the procedure of keeping a discipleship 'score', a policy I have implemented in Chasetown. (The label 'disciple' is simply a shorthand description for those who have continued to belong to the fellowship and is not necessarily an indicator of their level of commitment.)

St Thomas', Aldridge (1974–1986)

Year	No of teams	No of enquirers	No of commitments	No of disciples
1974	5	9†	3(43%†)	3(43%)
1975	19	33†	19(73%†)	14(54%)
1976	14	26†	16(70%†)	15(65%)
1977	11	21†	13(65%†)	11(55%)
1978	10	20†	12(71%†)	12(71%)
1979	7	13†	11(92%†)	7(58%)
1980	18	32†	21(68%†)	16(52%)
1981	36	58†	42(75%†)	27(48%)
1982	8	13	10(77%)	6(46%)
1983	20	31†	26(87%†)	18(60%)
1984	21	34	26(76%)	17(50%)
1985	21	28	15(58%)	13(46%)
1986	18	27†	14(52%†)	14(52%)
1987	14	22	17(77%)	8(36%)
1988 (Aug)	4	6	2(33%)	2(33%)
Total	**226**	**383**	**247(64%)**	**183(48%)**

† Some of those who did the course were already disciples—usually married to non-Christian spouses. They have been included in the figures in order to give an accurate picture of the total number of people who have done the course. However, they have been extracted from the figures for the purpose of calculating the percentages so as not to distort the true impact the course has made.

St Anne's, Chasetown (1981–1986)

Year	No of homes involved	No of enquirers involved	No of commitments	No of disciples
1981/2	11	21†	15(83%)	11(61%)
1983	9	15	13(87%)	11(73%)
1984	17	26†	20(95%)	13(62%)
1985	5	9	8(89%)	8(89%)
1986	19	37†	26(74%)	22(62%)
1987	6	11	7(63%)	6(55%)
1988 (Aug)	18	33†	14(52%)	13(48%)
Total	**85**	**152**	**103(75%)**	**84(62%)**

† See note to previous chart
In most cases the teams operated with a married couple, but it is clear from the figures that sometimes they went to one person on their own.

Perhaps the best way to bring the figures to life is simply to say that at St Thomas' eleven out of fifteen members of the present church committee came into the church in this way: the present treasurer, a churchwarden, two lay readers, a full-time pastoral assistant, numerous house group leaders, a candidate for Wycliffe Bible Translators, numerous Sunday School and youth leaders and leaders of uniformed organisations, not to mention the many who give their lives generously in the service of Christ and support those in positions of leadership.

At St Anne's, those who have come into the full life of the church through the outreach course include both churchwardens, six house group leaders, and seven who are teaching and leading in various departments of the Sunday School and young people's work. That means nearly a quarter have gone into active leadership positions, and there will be more to come. Half of those who became 'disciples' have been out themselves as members of teams at least once.

Of course it is not possible to guarantee that every convert will go on to become an active disciple, however careful we are to provide the best possible environment. The parable of the sower makes it clear that there will always be those who do not go on to produce fruit in their lives. It is always a source of disappointment when those who have made a Christian response drift away, for whatever reason, or fail to take any further step. It is important to keep in touch with them as far as possible, but in the end there is very little that can be done, other than to pray that the Spirit of God will stir them up and bring them to a point of deeper commitment either with us or with another fellowship.

NOTE

1   *Towards the Conversion of England* (London: 1945), p1.

CHAPTER TEN

THE ROLE OF THE MINISTER

'ANY FORWARD MOVE in evangelism must begin with the clergy themselves' states the report *Towards the Conversion of England*,[1] and it is certainly true that the Church of England badly needs an injection of people who have a vision for evangelism within the parish. I suspect that it is also true of *any* church that has a full-time ordained ministry as the focus of its leadership.

The personality of the minister is inevitably a major factor in the spiritual life of the local church. 'The spiritual temperature of a congregation depends chiefly on the parish priest.'[2] However far down the road of lay leadership a local church may have gone, it would be foolish to discount the importance of the person who is perceived by the community to be the focus of leadership of the local church. The minister's own personality and gifts will not only set the style of that ministry and leadership but will also contribute to the spiritual tone of the congregation. Whether we like it or not, the minister will be a crucial factor for good or ill in any evangelistic activity within the local church. Sadly, ministers often lag far behind their most dedicated and enthusiastic church members in their vision for evangelism, who then seek an outlet for their gifts in extra-parochial evangelistic enterprises while the local church slumbers on.

The question today is how much longer can the church slumber on? In many places, unless churches begin to make adult converts their future is likely to be bleak. The problem is that many ministers were not called or trained for a ministry in which evangelism had a high priority. Certainly within the Church of England most have been trained for a pastoral and teaching ministry. Now, that assumes the existence of a congregation that needs pastoring and teaching, a congregation which has largely grown up within the church. Ministers have been trained to nurture and care for a flock where children grow up into the faith and adult members of the congregation have a lifetime of church attendance behind them. Some of them would undoubtedly need converting, but it could be assumed that they would be familiar with biblical phraseology, and it was simply a case of the truth of what they already knew striking home to them in a personal way.

In how many places and for how much longer can the church continue to make that assumption? The Church of England has been a 'cradle' church for centuries; now it has to come to terms with the implications of becoming a 'convert' church. Nor is it alone in that respect. The German Roman Catholic theologian, Karl Rahner, saw the future of the church in Europe in terms of 'a little flock' within a dechristianised and pagan culture and emphasised the crucial importance of the church becoming a converting agency:

> The possibility of winning new Christians from a milieu that has become unchristian is the sole living and convincing evidence that even today Christianity still has a real chance for the future . . . It means more to win one new Christian from what we may call neo-paganism than to keep ten 'old Christians'.[3]

We have to take the winning of new converts seriously. Unless a church grows through adult converts it will be in danger of closing down.

Does this mean that all ministers must be evangelists? Of course not! However, the minister is concerned for the spiritual welfare of those under his charge and, within the Church of England at least that responsibility extends beyond the congregation to the wider parish community. Evangelism is therefore part of every minister's commission even if he or she has no personal gifts or inclinations in that direction. How then is that responsibility to be discharged?

I do not believe that every minister needs to be an evangelist in the sense of personally being the agent through whom people come to faith in Christ. In fact, the minister who is a skilled evangelist runs the risk of depriving the congregation of the privilege of exercising its own evangelistic gifts. It is always so much quicker, easier and more satisfying to do the job yourself! Had I possessed personal evangelistic gifts I wonder whether we would ever have devised our outreach strategy. As it is, I have no doubt that the most important medium for evangelism is the local church, and I see the minister's task as *mobilising and equipping the church* to become a converting agency. However, unless evangelism has a high priority on the minister's agenda as well as on the local church's agenda, it is unlikely that much of lasting value will be achieved.

The role of the minister in the particular outreach scheme we devised has been emerging as the story has unfolded. It is important for that role to be clearly understood by any churches proposing to use it, and I hope that the following observations will be of value.

Which homes?

As will already be clear from the examples quoted in earlier chapters, the minister is in a unique position to discover those homes that may be ready to receive a team. Such opportunities, of course, will not be confined to the minister, but in the early years of operating the scheme his or her participation at this level may well make the difference between success or failure. Unless the church leader gives it wholehearted support and is willing to approach pastoral contacts about receiving a team it will be much more difficult for the scheme to gain momentum. Consequently, interest among the church members will wane and it will be a case of yet another 'bright idea' tried and discarded. The personal recommendation of the minister counts for a lot in the eyes of people on the fringe or right outside the church. After all, their only encounter with such an approach will have been through the activity of the sects, and they will be understandably suspicious. They need to be reassured, and the best person to do that (at first) is the minister.

How, then, do you approach someone about receiving a team? If the offer is to stand any chance of being accepted you need to convey your own conviction that the people will benefit from it, that in no way will they be disappointed or feel that they have wasted their time, whatever the final outcome may be. A half-hearted, take-it-or-leave-it, it's-not-that-important approach is unlikely to gain much of a response. If you do not think it is worthwhile and are only making a token attempt to appease certain importunate church members, your lack of enthusiasm will hardly commend the idea to others. That is not to say that people should be pressured unfairly into doing something for which they have no real enthusiasm or for which they are not ready. Unless there is some evidence of the prior work of the Holy Spirit making them open to spiritual truth, the team will probably be wasting their time, even if they get an invitation.

In the early stages of launching the scheme it is important that the teams are not thrust into sterile and negative situations which will only sap their confidence. If they are being sent out to gather in the harvest (Lk 10:2), which is what the course is specifically designed to do, they should not be sent into places where there are barely a few green shoots above the ground. When Jesus sent out the seventy-two and 'they came back with great joy' (Lk 10:17), it was because he had instructed them clearly not to waste time in unproductive situations but to go where there was a harvest to be reaped.

To change the picture, young and inexperienced fishermen need the encouragement of actually catching fish! Too many fruitless fishing expeditions at that stage may dampen their enthusiasm for fishing altogether. It is the minister's responsibility to make sure that fishers of men go where the fish are biting. It is largely for that reason that I have always felt uneasy about making the course a *requirement* for (say) parents who want their children baptised.

If your church is in the blessed position of having plenty of experienced church members who can work with people who are doing the course not out of interest but simply as a means to an end, and if these members can cope with disappointment, then the course may be a useful preparation for baptism or other purposes. And, undoubtedly, even in the unpromising situation I have depicted, there will be some whose interest will be aroused as the course proceeds and who will come to faith. However, I would not recommend starting in that way without an exceptionally strong and mature congregation. I suspect most churches would struggle to raise even one or two people of the calibre required to persevere in such unpromising situations; most churches are like the two parishes where I have used the scheme—with people needing more than anything else the encouragement of actually catching fish.

The minister's first task, then, is to be alert to the opportunities; to assess the level of interest and to present the offer of a team in as attractive a way as possible; then to stand back and let the team go to work.

What matter that sometimes the fish cannot wait to jump into your net! Like Melvyn, who wanted to know how to 'get Jesus into his life'—his actual words; or Mike and Di, who turned up in church one day, obviously searching for a deeper meaning to life; or Anju, a Hindu lady, hungry for a personal relationship with God. Of course, it would be possible for the minister to deal with them personally, but how much better that members of the congregation should have that joy and privilege! It does wonders for their faith, renews their confidence in the power of God, and encourages them to speak more freely of their Lord!

Which teams?

The task of team selection will then require attention. The minister is likely to be the person in the best position to know which members of the congregation will relate well to those who have requested a team. Of course, the more teams that need to be fielded, the more time consuming is the process, and there are not really any short-cuts. Each situation will demand prayerful appraisal. I have found a simple chart listing members' availability some help (see sample page 122), but even then each person has to be contacted before the team can be finalised. If possible, it is helpful to consult with at least one other person about your team selection, just in case you have overlooked any factor that would make the team's task more difficult. Clearly it needs to be someone with a good knowledge of the congregation and a certain amount of discernment—a longstanding deacon, elder or church warden may well fit the bill.

My normal procedure has been to work out what I think are the best teams for the various homes, then ask my wife what she thinks with her own knowledge of the church members. When she has vetoed this—('You couldn't possibly send him out on the same team as her! Didn't you know that . . .') and rearranged that, for reasons I had not taken into account, we then discuss the merits of each team and arrive at our final selection. Then just as we are breathing a sigh of relief at having solved the jigsaw puzzle, the phone rings and one of the key people we had been counting on to lead a team tells us he won't be available because his firm wants him to go abroad suddenly, or they have just changed his shift at the factory, or his long awaited hospital appointment has arrived, or his widowed mother has been taken ill etc. So back to the drawing board we go juggling with a new set of permutations in order to plug the gap. Eventually, after a lot of prayer and discussion and holding of breath, all the teams are ready to start.

All that remains is to inform everyone involved. A simple slip giving the names, addresses and telephone numbers of team members and hosts, and the date and time of starting, makes sure that there are no misunderstandings. We recommend team leaders to deliver these to their team members personally and to the home they will be visiting. This gives them the chance to say a friendly 'hello' a week or so before they arrive with the team.

Unless there are any particular pastoral problems in the home they are visiting, such as a recent bereavement, or a domestic difficulty, or an involvement with the occult, or contact with the spiritualist church or one of the sects, I only give the briefest details to the team leader so that the team goes in on a normal footing and behaves naturally. Even in the situations I have mentioned I will only give the minimum of information needed for the teams to avoid causing unwitting hurt or embarrassment. I brief them carefully about preserving confidentiality.

Once the course begins the minister is available as a resource person to the teams and a trouble-shooter if anything goes wrong. Only once have I needed to go into a situation, on the invitation of the team leader, to help resolve an area of real tension in a home—and that is one home out of two hundred that have received teams. Usually any questions or difficulties that arise can be handled by the team, although they will sometimes need to seek guidance or advice from the minister or elders about how best to proceed. In most cases the teams do not need to have recourse to the minister at all, but it is important that they do not feel abandoned. It is an encouragement to them to know that the minister is interested in how they are progressing and the occasional casual enquiry in that direction just lets them know that they are not forgotten!

When the course has been completed I like to pay a personal visit to the home. The visit need not be a lengthy one, unless the people have matters they want to discuss, but it does provide an invaluable opportunity to review the value the course has been to them and the impression that the team has made. This applies equally whether they have made a personal commitment to Christ or not. If they have said 'no' it can help them to know that the church has been grateful for the opportunity to share the gospel with them and hopes that the links with them will continue and grow.

On one or two occasions teams have reported back that they felt strongly that the couple wanted to become Christians but hadn't quite had the courage to take that step, and a visit from me might clinch matters for them. So it was with Rob and Sheila. I happened to call on them the day after they had moved into the area, and the contacts developed from there. They began to attend the monthly family service and eventually invited a team to their home. Rob didn't think

Chart as used at St Thomas', Aldridge in 1976

Members available	Mon	Tues	Wed	Thurs	Fri
Jeremy	x		x	x	x
Sue	x	x		x	
Ann	x	x	x	x	
Daphne	x				
Erica	x				
David			x	x	
Christine			x		
Rose	x	x	x	x	
Brenda		x	x	x	x
Bob		x	x	x	
Ken				x	x
Jean			x	x	x
Brian			x		
Frank			x		
Eric		x	x	x	x
Tim	x	x	x	x	
Joyce			x		x
Margaret			x		
Muriel			x	x	
Robin	x		x	x	x
Pat	x	x	x		
Roy	x	x	x	x	
Carol	x			x	
Chris	x	x	x	x	x
Sylvia	x	x	x		
Stephanie			x		
Heather			x		
Pauline	x	x	x		
Alison		x			
Bob			x	x	
Mary			x	x	

Homes to visit

	Mon	Tues	Wed	Thurs	Fri
1 Lynette & Martin	x		x		x
2 Lynda & David	x			x	x
3 Arax	x	x	x	x	x
4 Ann & Kevin			x	x	
5 Deirdre & Jim	x	x			
6 Dennis & Gloria	x				
7 Martin			x		

Christianity was for him; he didn't have the right sort of accent! He came from a typical working-class background and didn't think he was 'good enough' to be a Christian. He agreed reluctantly to sit in on the course to please Sheila. 'Initially I was very anti,' he confessed later, 'but at the end of the course I realised that there was a God.'

However, when the team asked about a personal commitment, he was happy for Sheila to go ahead, but did not feel able to do so himself. So I called round to talk things through with him one evening. It became clear as we talked that there were no major stumbling blocks to his becoming a Christian. He was simply looking for a degree of certainty that is unobtainable before making a decision for Christ. I used the analogy of marriage to make the point: just as you cannot be absolutely certain that the person you propose to marry is the right one—there is an element of risk involved in any such relationship—so you can never be one hundred per cent certain about God before taking the risk of committing yourself to him. If you wait until you are one hundred per cent certain you never get married; and it is similar when it comes to a relationship with God. We talked at length. When I left I asked him to let me know when he had taken the final step. I did not have to wait long. He rang me the next day with the good news.

ALL AMATEURS, STAND UP!

In this chapter I have tried to draw out the main areas in which I see the minister having an important role to play. However, none of these things has to be done by the minister, or by the minister alone. Every church situation will be different. Certainly, in the average church, with a congregation of between fifty and a hundred and fifty, his or her involvement as motivator or enabler will be essential until the scheme is well established. If there are members of the congregation in a better position than the minister to do these tasks and with the time available to take them on, or at least share the load, that is all to the good. In the long term it is vital that the scheme is owned and operated by the church members, so that when the minister moves on, the evangelistic outreach continues.

There is one area in which the minister should certainly *not* be involved, and that is as a team member. This is work for 'amateurs' not 'the professional'! It is best done by those who do it for the love of it. However 'laid back' or in touch with the people the minister may take pride in being, when it comes to discussing matters of faith, he or she is still the 'professional', not only in the sense of being paid, but more important, in the sense of being trained and educated. In anything but academic or student circles that is a considerable disadvantage.

The minister will inevitably be an inhibiting factor, both to the hosts and to fellow team members. Who would feel free to say what they really thought about God, the Church or its leaders with the minister himself or herself sitting there?

Who would be brave enough to ask certain questions with the 'professional' present? No one likes to appear ignorant or foolish. Yet it is vital that people can say exactly what they think, especially in their own homes, because it is often these suppressed feelings that are a stumbling block to their really hearing the Christian message. While those feelings remain unexpressed, they clutter up their hearts and minds.

But the minister will also inhibit the other members of the team. They will hesitate to say things for fear of revealing their own ignorance, or saying the wrong thing and having the embarrassment of being corrected in public. They may also want the minister to take the lead and do all the work.

And what about those tricky questions when they arise? Who will handle those? The minister, of course! Hence the team members may easily find themselves in a passive role, happy to nod agreement with everything the minister says, but thereby deprived of the need to exercise faith. Instead of growing through the experience of being exposed to questions or problems to which they have no easy answers; instead of having to pray for instant wisdom and guidance, and thereby discovering that Jesus' promise: 'do not worry beforehand what you are going to say; when the time comes, say whatever is then given to you. For the words you speak will not be yours; they will come from the Holy Spirit' (Mk 13:11) was not just for first century disciples; instead of facing those challenges and experiencing the power of God at work—they can sit back and enjoy a pleasant evening secure in the knowledge that the minister has it all under control.

The minister is best left out of the teams. Having said all that, if the *only* way to start is for the minister to take out two lay people, then that is how it must be; God has a way of compensating for the disadvantage!

Only when the scheme had been operating for three years and the pattern had been well established did I venture onto a team. We were particularly hard pressed at that time. It was a source of amusement and encouragement to the church members that I had to report a negative response at the end of the course!

NOTES

1   (London:1945), p11.
2   *Ibid*, p40.
3   *The Shape of the Church to Come* (SPCK:London, 1974), p32ff.

CHAPTER ELEVEN

GROWING ON

ONE SUNDAY MORNING when the sun was shining brightly and I wasn't busy in the vestry with last-minute arrangements for the family service, I decided to stand outside the main door of the church centre and greet people as they arrived. The church centre was the geographical hub of the estate, which was criss-crossed with walkways, all converging on the church like the spokes of a wheel. (It was one of those back-to-front estates with service roads running to the rear of the houses.)

The sight that met my eyes is still vividly printed on my mind. There was a queue stretching some thirty or forty yards back from the church doors, with people happily chatting in the sunshine, and yet others streaming along the walkways from every direction. When I expressed my amazement to the churchwardens, they didn't turn a hair. It was always like that on family service morning, they assured me. Normally I only saw the crowds when they were inside the building—packed wall to wall. We had a comfortable seating capacity of 250, but for family services we had to bring in extra benches for the children to sit on, so that we often had nearer three hundred and fifty crammed in. I had never thought what all those people looked like as they arrived for church. It was certainly an uplifting sight, and I wondered what impact it had on our unchurched neighbours to see people actually queueing to get in when there was so much talk of the Church being in decline!

In the September of 1979 St Thomas' celebrated its tenth anniversary. It was an opportunity not only to look back, but more importantly, to take stock and look positively towards the future. In the preparations for those celebrations, all the strands that had gone into the establishing of the Church Centre and its growth to the present—many of them unknown to the majority of the congregation—were brought out and drawn together. They helped greatly to give a sense of identity to what was still only a church in its infancy. In a rapidly growing church, such opportunities are valuable.

Cabbages?

When we had embarked on our outreach strategy five years earlier, one of our stated aims was that outreach should continue and become a normal part of church life. At that point we had not seriously considered the long-term implications of such a strategy in any realistic way. We were just excited about setting out on a venture of faith. We saw a population of six thousand and all the possibilities for evangelism, but we had not thought through how we would cope if we reached only ten per cent of the people in the area!

However, in 1977 I had come across a 48-page duplicated workpaper called 'Divide and Conquer' put out by the Rev David Wasdell.[1] It was the sub-title—'Towards the Multi-centre Parish'—that caught my attention. I was intrigued and enthralled as I read. The paper sprang from a sociological and statistical analysis of Anglican parishes, but the theological and practical implications he drew from them were what excited me. A paragraph headed 'Our dammed church'[2] described the situation facing the church in graphic terms:

> One of the most important facts to surface from recent research into parish life has been the in-built numerical limitation of its membership, which is inherent in the traditional structure of the parish organisation. Just as a cabbage, a tomato, a swarm of bees or a human being has an optimum size, so does a congregation. Individual cabbages may vary in size within certain limits. Those limits may be affected by the amount of fertiliser in the soil, the kind of cabbage, the amount of attention it gets, rainfall,

sunlight and a host of other parameters—but limited the cabbage is. It doesn't just grow and grow. No matter how big the field in which the cabbage is planted, it doesn't change the limit to its size.

Like it or not, the fact of the self-limiting congregation is there, staring us in the face.

His research in 1975 had revealed that the traditional pattern of one man, one building imposed a limit on growth which meant that once a church had an average membership of around 175 it ceased to grow. Adding new members to a church of that size was counter-productive. Adding another minister to the team increased the ceiling by one hundred only, on average, so a law of diminishing returns begins to set in. (His more recent research, as yet unpublished, reveals that the optimum size for such a congregation now varies around an average of about 154.)

I had never thought about the characteristics and limitations of different sizes of groups in any systematic way. Observations like the following on evangelism struck home with considerable force:

> The privilege of sharing the good news with a neighbour is a privilege vested in the whole Body of Christ. To omit evangelism from the mission of the church is to mutilate its ministry, and to deny to the world the opportunity of wholeness of being in relationship with God, the provision of which cost Christ so dear. Now, to be effective, any evangelistic effort must be backed by the provision of welcoming places within the community of the Body of Christ, holes in which new members can easily fit, and in which they can grow in faith and understanding, participation, maturity and service.
>
> One of the most disturbing effects of the self-limiting congregation is that its ability to welcome the newcomers decreases with the rise in membership. When the congregation is operating at its dynamic ceiling, no amount of evangelistic motivation, campaigns, or calls to mission can create permanent growth in the local congregation.[3]

It would appear that our vision of continuous evangelism was going to run into unforeseen difficulties. At some point, in the not too distant future, we were going to face a crisis, if David Wasdell was right.

The effects of this in-built counter-evangelistic factor in congregational life are devastating . . . the congregation finds itself caught in a double bind—aware of its obligations in mission, yet even more deeply aware that if mission were to go forward, the old depth and quality of congregational life upon which the maintenance of membership hangs, would be threatened. So members find themselves moving in two ways at once—attempting to make new Christians, and yet also attempting to defend the boundaries of the congregation.[4]

His conclusion was inexorable: 'If evangelism is to be effective, if mission is to survive, then congregational structures must be so reformed that they remain open to new members, however many are involved.' I hoped he had some constructive ideas about how that could be achieved, or our vision of continuous growth would be in jeopardy!

I was still reeling under the impact of that thought as I read on—to discover that it wasn't just the congregation who would have problems as the church grew. Growth would create all sorts of problems and pressures for me, the minister:

As numbers of people per parish rise, so the available pastoral care per person decreases. To start with the pastor simply gets busier, but he eventually reaches his work peak and from then on the pastoral function of the Anglican parish begins to break down. Pastoral care then becomes inevitably selective; some receiving more attention than others, and the distinction is made between congregational members and non-attending parishioners. The more members of the congregation there are, the more they have to compete with each other for the pastor's attention and time. A certain amount of jealousy and envy gets built in. Particular personality types may find a weakness in the pastor's defences and use it to gain a disproportionate amount of his time. Care becomes geared to crisis rather than promotion of growth, and once the crisis is passed the person is dropped as some new crisis presents itself to the pastor's attention. Hopes and expectations are raised only to be dashed again. Disappointment, resentment and bitterness build up.[5]

What had we let ourselves in for when we set off with such enthusiasm on our evangelistic strategy? David Wasdell was building a very good case, in my mind, for some pretty radical action. I read on in anticipation. His solution was clear and unequivocal:

> It has become crystal clear that the strategy of growth by addition of new members to existing groups or congregations is self-defeating. As numbers increase, so the quality of life which sustains the group is destroyed. Opportunities for personal learning, participation and maturation, pastoral care, taking of responsibility and use of gifts, all begin to disappear. While the church retains this strategy of growth by addition she stands firmly in the way of the purpose of God for the wholeness of man.
>
> Now, there would appear to be only one alternative to growth by addition, and that is growth by multiplication. In other words, once we have seen the folly of trying to grow small groups into big groups, and big groups into crowds, and have had the courage to say that sustaining small groups, and keeping them as small groups, is essential for the very life of the church, then growth must be through the multiplication of smaller groups.[6]

If our evangelism continued to be as effective as it had been already, we clearly had to take David Wasdell's contention seriously, and sooner rather than later. I saw it as so crucial that 'Divide and Conquer' was required reading for every member of the church council.

Multiplying and dividing

We discussed it at some length and with considerable profit. We were unanimous that such a plan was the only way forward, however difficult it might be to carry out. We were aware that it would require a great deal of re-thinking from church members used to familiar patterns of church life, but what alternative was there? Continuous growth was proving to be more complicated than I had realised!

In a newsletter to church members in September 1977 the church committee shared some of its thinking with them and launched the idea of the 'multi-centre parish'. We had used homes for meetings on many occasions, and small groups were part of people's experience; but this was a far more radical approach. These groups would be a permanent part of the organisational life of the church, not an optional extra for those who enjoyed small groups.

Had anyone in the country tried to make it work? A phone call to David Wasdell elicited the information that he knew of only one person who had been working along these lines long enough to be able to help us—the Revd Robert Warren at St Thomas', Crookes, Sheffield. Would he be willing to come and share his experience with us? I asked Robert over the telephone. Back came the suggestion that we should come to Sheffield and see the groups in action. They could accomodate up to sixty people for a weekend. We would stay in the homes of group members, and that would give us the opportunity to join in the life of the groups as well as discuss with leaders and members the theological and practical outworkings of their plan.

In the event, twenty-four of us spent a weekend in November with the congregation of St Thomas', Crookes. We were encouraged and challenged by the warmth of fellowship and the level of commitment exhibited by the church members. There was a degree of personal and financial sacrifice which opened our eyes. They freely opened their homes to others and gave up family holiday money to help support the church. Some people even took on extra jobs to help out financially. But they did not hide from us the pitfalls and the pressures involved in working out new structures of this sort. We returned with a much clearer vision of how such a programme could be implemented and with a keen awareness of what it might cost in personal terms. What we saw in Sheffield were not cosy Christian discussion groups, but people seeking to work out their Christian faith in a sort of extended family, sharing belongings as well as time with each other, involved in caring for neighbours and sharing their faith with them, finding strength from one another within the group through prayer and a shared vision. That visit changed our perception of what a network of Christian cells might entail and could achieve under God, for all its shortcomings. We came back knowing that this was the direction we had to move in.

The key to this strategy was a network of cell groups organised on a geographical basis, so that each group was a microcosm of the church in its own area. Now clearly small groups have their limitations. Certain functions cannot really be sustained by the church in the home in isolation from the rest of the body. Inspirational and celebratory worship, major community action, a viable youth work are all obvious examples.

The small groups must not be seen as complete in themselves, but as subunits of the wider church, without which they could not survive. It would be vital to foster a sense of mutual interdependence between the groups, by creating a structure that enabled each group to see the importance of its relationship to all the others as members of the Body of Christ.

David Wasdell expressed this most helpfully in an article entitled 'Long Range Planning and the Church' which contained the diagram opposite and comment.

> Members find their fundamental point of belonging within a small group of 8–12 people and as new members are added so new groups are formed. As the number of cells increase they are drawn together into clusters involving some 60–120 people.[7]

The result of this is to free the congregation from the normal limitations of size which arise when new members continue to be added to a single unit congregation under one minister.

We knew that the plan wouldn't be as simple as it sounds on paper. We were well aware of the risks in such an enterprise. We were also aware of the demands that would be made on cell group leaders, and the difficulty of finding suitable people to take on that responsibility. We were a congregation of predominantly 'young' Christians, and it takes time to grow leaders who can carry pastoral responsibilities with maturity. We were also conscious that we would continue to need people to lead and run outreach teams, the demand for which showed no sign of abating. Yet, what choice did we have? If we delayed too long in carrying out such a plan we would reach our optimum size as a congregation and growth would peter out, leaving us becalmed in complacency with a comfortably full church each Sunday. Once that sort of inertia has set in, it is very difficult to motivate people for evangelism, and any radical restructuring is fiercely resisted.

Alternative Social System

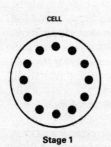

CELL

Stage 1

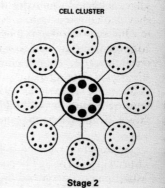

CELL CLUSTER

Stage 2

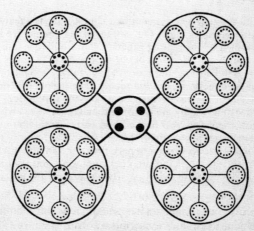

FEDERATION OF
CLUSTERS

Stage 3

So it was that we launched our first house fellowship groups in January 1978 with ninety people. They did not all prove to be an unqualified success, but we had no hesitation in persevering with them. They were vital as the congregation continued to grow through the use of the outreach scheme. They meant that new Christians had somewhere they belonged on a deeper level than was possible in a growing congregation.

However, by the autumn of 1979, it was also becoming abundantly clear that we would have to do something about extending our church buildings. We had taken the precaution of obtaining outline planning permission for such an eventuality as early as 1977 while carrying out two small improvements to the buildings, but it was the visit of the Revd. Eddie Gibbs that made us more aware of its importance.

In November he led a Bible Society day conference on church growth at St Thomas', in the course of which he drew attention to overcrowding as a limiting factor in church growth. I had been rejoicing to see people queuing to get into church and having difficulty in finding a seat when they did get inside and had not thought about the long-term consequences.

> The most dangerous moment in a church's life is when the last remaining seat is filled. Our notion of maximum size is often determined by the seating capacity of our building. The size of our plant limits the scope of our vision. As soon as the church becomes full on a regular basis and overfull on festival and other special occasions, frustration sets in. The people who are most conscious of the inconveniences are not the committed 'saints', who are more highly motivated and make sure they arrive early to park their cars and find a good seat. Those who are most frustrated are the marginal, shall we/shan't we? contingent; it is they who turn up too late to park their car and find a seat.
>
> The time to tackle this problem is not when you are 100% full and in danger of decline, but when you are 80% full and still rising![8]

The matter was made more pressing by the fact that we already had ten homes requiring teams in January 1980 and were committed to active participation in a Bible Society inspired distribution of gospels to every home in the Metropolitan Borough of Walsall, of which Aldridge formed a part. It was planned to start immediately after Easter. 'Good News for Aldridge' presented a marvellous opportunity to visit every home in our area with a positive purpose.

We anticipated a good number of openings for our outreach teams as a result. Nor were we to be disappointed. Six homes wanted teams in the autumn, and a further twenty were required for the following January! We realised that we had to grasp the nettle of extending the church premises without delay and opened discussions with the architect in September 1980. In November we had costings for three alternatives—all of which were far more than we could afford.

Could we look into the possibility of the work being done under a Manpower Services Commission scheme? The Glebe Centre in Walsall had a large and successful scheme skilfully managed by the Revd Ted Littlejohn. Discussions with him resulted in the unanimous approval of the church council that we should use a team of unemployed young people for this work. In a free and frank exchange between the church council and Ted Littlejohn, we thrashed out the realities of what would be involved. It was clear that it would not result in a large financial saving; and it might cause us considerable inconvenience.

The architect was certainly not very happy! He would not be dealing with professionals in the way to which he was accustomed, and he was understandably perturbed. However, in the light of a bad—and worsening—unemployment situation, we felt it right to take the risks the architect had pointed out to us. The financial saving would be small because the job would take two or three times as long to complete, and in a time of rapid inflation the cost of building materials was almost impossible to calculate from month to month. However, it would have the advantage to us that we would not have to pay the bills so quickly, and we would be able to raise the capital as we went along.

We set our sights on Easter 1981 for the work to begin. Easter came and went. The financial target we had set ourselves had not been met; the Glebe Centre had not managed to recruit a team; and some of us were beginning to get cold feet about the whole undertaking. On 22nd June, after putting the matter to the whole church, the committee met to pray and then vote by secret ballot. Unless there was a unanimous decision, we would go no further. All fifteen members of the committee, some of whom had expressed considerable misgivings, voted in favour of proceeding. Work began on site on 16th July. Ann and I already knew that we would not be there to see the building to completion.

NOTES

1 David Wasdell, 'Divide and Conquer: Towards the Multi-centre Parish' (The Urban Church Project, 1975). Used with permission.
2 *Ibid*, p4.
3 *Ibid*, p10.
4 *Ibid*.
5 *Ibid*, p11.
6 *Ibid*, p19.
7 David Wasdell, 'Long-Range Planning and the Church' *Long-Range Planning*, vol 13, no 3 (1980). Used with permission.
8 Eddie Gibbs, *Body-Building Exercises for the Local Church* (Falcon: London, 1979), pp45—46.

CHAPTER TWELVE

MOVING ON

IT WAS IN EARLY JANUARY 1981, when we were totally
immersed in getting twenty teams into action and nego-
tiating about the much-needed extension to the church,
that we received a phone call from the Bishop of
Wolverhampton. Did I know that the parish of Chasetown
was becoming vacant at the end of March, and would I
consider the possibility of moving there?

We *had* already heard about Chasetown and the coming
departure of their vicar. In fact, I knew quite a bit about the
parish in an indirect fashion. In my capacity as a lay reader
tutor responsible for taking potential readers through a
three-year training course, I had come to know four of the lay
readers in Chasetown very well. They had only completed
their training six months before the bombshell came. Bill
Woods had been in Chasetown just four years and one of the
first things he had done was to encourage them to go forward
for training. Now he was leaving, and they were afraid
that all the good work he had begun might run into the
sand.

All four came from the Mission Church in the parish
situated in the district known as Chase Terrace. St John's
had been the 'Cinderella' church for many years, but it had
really begun to blossom under Bill's ministry as he
encouraged lay initiative and evangelism. The readers were
all actively involved in the running of the little church with
Bill's wholehearted approval. Hence their concern. The

news of his intended departure had cast a cloud over the approaching Christmas celebrations.

Ann and I tried to encourage them to pray positively that God would call the right person to build on Bill's work and not destroy it—little dreaming at that time that it might be us! We had no plans to move at that stage. But we did wonder whether we would be approached and what we would say if we were.

Six months before, when I had been at St Thomas', Aldridge for seven years, the bishop had already sounded me out about the future, and I had expressed an interest in moving to a more working-class area. I wanted an opportunity to see whether the outreach scheme would work there, or whether it was only suitable for articulate middle-class people, as some had inferred. I had also told him that I felt committed to St Thomas' for at least another year. Now that the building project was going to be under the auspices of the Manpower Services Commission, that commitment seemed even more binding.

Even before my discussion with the bishop, Ann and I had talked about the strategic time to move and were clear in our own minds that the growth of the work at St Thomas' meant that we either had to move in about twelve months time or commit ourselves to a further five years. When the phone call came we had mentally committed ourselves to seeing through the building project, so that whoever followed would be able to concentrate on the next phase in the growth of the church. It did not seem to be a good time to move when the building would be only half-completed and the money to pay for it still to be found. Who would want to come into such a situation? And if there were a long gap between our leaving and the next person coming it would put a terrific strain on the very busy lay leadership. We knew that the average length of time for an interregnum in the diocese was six months, and we could not easily envisage abandoning them in the middle of a rather complicated building project.

I explained my reservations to the bishop and pressed him closely about the importance of the move from his standpoint. I certainly did not want to move just to fill a vacancy.

In our conversation six months previously he had mentioned that there might be a number of possibilities when the time came to leave Aldridge. Was Chasetown the place he really wanted me to go to?

His answer was unequivocal: 'It is. Will you give it some consideration?'

I could hardly refuse. After all, bishops in the Church of England are as much part of the process of God's guidance as common sense, inner conviction, prayer and prophetic utterances. Furthermore, my assessment of what was in the best interests of St Thomas' might not be the same as God's, even if I might feel bad about leaving at the 'wrong' time.

Needless to say, it was not with a great deal of enthusiasm or conviction that Ann and I went to talk with Bill and Margaret Woods one cold January day. We came back slightly relieved. Nothing that we saw or heard moved us to feel that we were right for Chasetown or that Chasetown was right for us. Unfortunately, neither did we come away feeling that it was completely out of the question, so we still had to take seriously the fact that the bishop, whose judgement we respected, wanted us to go there.

As Bill was not leaving until March there was no pressure for a quick decision, so we shelved it for a while hoping that time would bring some clarity, but it didn't. It was obvious that we could not delay for ever, so we set the end of February as a deadline. If we did not have any more positive conviction by then, we would have to say no. As yet, we had not talked to the churchwardens of the parish. We arranged to meet them in Chasetown on 27th February, our son's eighth birthday.

We liked David and Richard immediately. Both in their late twenties, they made us feel quite old! It was their third year in office and they were refreshingly frank and open. They had taken soundings and were armed with a comprehensive list of questions. As they worked through the description of the sort of person the parish required, Ann and I looked at each other in amused acceptance. It matched in every respect the particular gifts that the lay leaders at St Thomas' had told us we exercised in our ministry. It was almost as if David and Richard had somehow got hold of the results of the gifts discernment exercise to which we had so recently submitted ourselves and written their job description around it! We had prayed for clear guidance, and we had no doubt that we had received it.

We reported back to the wardens at St Thomas', who had been praying with us for a clear outcome to the meeting. Together we concluded that if the Lord wanted us in Chasetown he wouldn't leave St Thomas' out of his purposes, however inconvenient the move would be for them on the human level. That conviction proved to be well-founded. Before our departure from Aldridge on 16th August, with the footings for the church extension barely dug, we knew that the Rev David Butterfield would be licensed as the new minister on 22nd September—hardly time for people to notice that we had gone!

Chasing around Chasetown

Although Chasetown is only five miles from Aldridge, it is in a different deanery and relates to a different group of parishes. Despite our connections with the lay readers, we had never had much reason to go there. Standing in the triangle formed by Brownhills to the south, Cannock to the West and Lichfield to the east, it isn't really on the road to anywhere. I had only been there twice before the bishop's phone call.

The first time was by accident, one dark winter's evening, soon after coming to Aldridge. I had been asked to preach at a St John's Church in a place called Heath Hayes just a couple of miles from Chase Terrace. I had been given clear instructions how to find the church and hadn't bothered to check by daylight precisely where it was. I hadn't bargained for how confusing the area was, especially after dark. I got lost a couple of times, then to my relief, with ten minutes to spare, a church building loomed up, and the notice board announced that it was in fact St John's. I thought the churchwarden looked at me rather curiously as I hurried through the door to greet the lay reader who was already robed, ready for the service. He looked at me in astonishment as I introduced myself as the visiting preacher. They already had one visiting preacher in the vestry! I was at the wrong St John's. 'This is St John's, Chase Terrace,' he explained to my dismay. I did eventually find the right St John's, and I was only ten minutes late!

My only other visit had been to a meeting in someone's home for people from all the churches. I had been invited to go with some members from St Thomas' to talk about the outreach course which we had begun to use with good effect. My only recollection is that the house was crammed with people and the ensuing discussion could have gone on for a very long time. I would never have been able to find the house again without a guide.

Even when we moved there I found it totally baffling as an area. It had no central point from which you could get your bearings. There were three distinct communities— Chasetown, Chase Terrace, and Burntwood—which had been merged into one by an extensive programme of building, so that you could no longer tell where one began and the other ended. The confusion was compounded by the fact that the three communities together made up the local authority parish of Burntwood.

Here you really could be in two places at once, except that you might not be quite where you thought you were. The poor unsuspecting traveller looking for Burntwood Shopping Centre will find it in Chase Terrace, while the visitor to the Burntwood Recreation Centre would find it in Chasetown (and Burntwood, of course,) and not at all in Burntwood as he might have thought! The result is total bewilderment. But that is not all, for part of what the unsuspecting visitor would think is Chasetown (or Burntwood), is in fact in the parish of Hammerwich—a village more than a mile away, hidden from view by rolling farmland! Add to that a Walsall postal address and you have a splendid recipe for chaos. It is the sort of strategy you would employ in war-time to confuse the enemy! It is not surprising that Burntwood, in its wider sense, is a community without a clear identity, except in political terms.

My responsibility was to be the parish of Chasetown, with its parish church of St Anne, built in 1865, and its mission church of St John, in Chase Terrace, built in 1886.

Both communities had only come into existence in the nineteenth century with the discovery of coal in the area. For over a hundred years coal was mined in Chasetown and Chase Terrace by the Cannock Chase Colliery Company, then the National Coal Board. The last pits closed in the 1960s at the same time as new estates began to be built to meet the demand of people from the West Midlands conurbation for more desirable residences away from the urban centres.

The housing was cheap enough to attract first-time buyers and those in the lower income brackets. This invasion of 'Brummies', who soon outnumbered the local residents, met with resentment and hostility by many. By the time the building was completed, the parish population was over 14,000, while the population of Burntwood as a whole reached nearly 30,000. However, despite the influx of newcomers, the local communities still retain their identities, at least in the minds of those born and bred in the area.

The simple enquiry 'Are you a local person?' may elicit the reply: 'Yes, *I* am. But my husband's from Chase Terrace'—or Burntwood, as the case may be. Yet they may not have been brought up more than half a mile from each other!

A depressing picture?

St Anne's is a large Victorian building which originally seated six hundred people. Built by the local mine owner, John Robinson McClean, for the benefit of his employees, it was designed by Edward Adams in a Byzantine style which is quite striking. From the outside the building is very drab and unprepossessing, but the interior design is most unusual. It also has the distinction, I discovered, of being one of the earliest churches in the world to be lit by electricity—the power coming from the nearby number 2 pit.

However, my first impression, when I came to an evening service incognito soon after Bill Woods' departure, was so depressing that I left after the Third Collect, wondering what on earth I had let myself in for. After the warmth and intimacy of St Thomas', the church was vast, cold, damp and badly-lit, full of dark-stained pitch pine pews and furniture, all set off by faded paintwork. The few people in the congregation, outnumbered by the distant choir hiding in the chancel, were scattered about in one's and two's. It was every cartoonist's impression of Anglican worship. I knew I wouldn't be able to live with that for long!

St John's, by contrast, was a typical Victorian mission church with seating for about 120. Perhaps its most striking feature was the extraordinary colour scheme—a combination of blue, pink and buttercup yellow walls—chosen, I was told, by a colour-blind churchwarden! At least it was warm and intimate. There was a family feel to the congregation, as there often is in that size of building. It was a growing congregation under largely lay leadership. In those surroundings I was surprised to find a fully robed choir leading the worship. It struck me as rather incongruous as they struggled up the narrow aisle in single file trying to look dignified, but for the church members it was undoubtedly a way of declaring that they were a 'proper' church within the Anglican tradition.

I knew from the lay readers I had trained that Bill Woods had been trying to find a curate for the parish for several years without success. I was assured that I could have a curate—if I could find one! There was a house available in the parish; but it couldn't have been in a worse place. It stood, empty and forlorn, on the opposite side of the road to the vicarage. What curate in his right mind would want to live that close to his vicar? In any case, a curate needed to be based in Chase Terrace, not Chasetown. I saw no point in looking for anyone until a suitable house was available. If I were to have any chance of finding a colleague by the time I arrived in the parish at the end of August, the house must be sold as quickly as possible. David and Richard were in total agreement and conveyed my request to the church council. They would also have to begin negotiations with the diocese for the purchase of a house in Chase Terrace as close to St John's as possible. It would be no easy task to find a suitable property. There were very few houses in Chase Terrace of the right size.

Only a couple of months later I received a phone call from one of the lay readers at St John's to say that they had just heard that the Scripture Union worker for the Midlands, who lived in Chase Terrace, was expecting to move in the summer and would be putting his house on the market quite soon. He lived less than 400 yards from the church and he had added a study extension onto the house! A phone call confirmed that he would be delighted if we purchased the house from him for that purpose and would not put it on the open market. Only two questions remained. Would the house pass muster with the diocesan surveyor? And would the diocese lend us the money to bridge the gap between the selling price of the old curate's house and the purchase price of the new one?

That the house was not ideal, but that it was adequate, was the verdict of the surveyor. Yet there was even better news on the financial front! The diocese had recently adopted the policy of purchasing houses for curates and charging an annual rental to the parish. So we would not need a loan at all; and the money from the sale of the other house would be ours to invest. The church council could hardly believe it!

JONATHAN AND FAITH

The search for a curate was not at first so successful. I was looking for someone who already had parish experience and could take over responsibility for St John's without too much supervision, leaving me free to get to grips with the main parish church. When July came and went with no one in sight I resigned myself to running the parish on my own for a year. Then, out of the blue, the Bishop of Lichfield rang. He had a young man and his family with him. They had been looking at a possible first curacy in Lichfield, but it hadn't worked out. Could I see them the next day before they returned to Nottingham, as he thought they might fit Chasetown? So it was that Ann and I met Jonathan and Faith Fox, with their twin boys Timothy and Andrew, in the empty vicarage in Chasetown.

Faith sat on the only chair. The rest of us perched on window ledges. We had no means of making tea or coffee. It was certainly not a text-book interviewing situation! The twins were understandably fractious; Faith looked worn out, and Jonathan did his best to carry on an intelligent conversation. But by the time we all left I had formed a favourable impression. I didn't know, however, whether the curacy would appeal to them; it wouldn't be a normal first curacy, and they certainly wouldn't get very much supervision. We would both be starting in a new parish within a few weeks of each other, and I would have my work cut out just to keep abreast of the parish church. They would be thrown in the deep end and would have to learn the hard way. The work would not appeal to everyone.

When I wrote to them a few days later offering them the post, I wondered what their response would be. I need not have worried. They took up the challenge.

David and Richard were keen for me to meet the church council before my arrival in Chasetown, and a visit was arranged for July. By then I had begun to form a clear idea of what was required in the parish and was able to alert them to what they should expect. My knowledge of the parish was such that I would not need to spend six months assessing the situation before setting a direction for the work.

Bill Woods' ministry, I knew, had brought new life and new people into St Anne's, but it had also stirred up considerable opposition and even personal hostility. The changes he had introduced had upset some of the long-standing members of the church. There was a lack of understanding between the newcomers and the traditionalists, and that tension was evident below the surface at that meeting of the church council. In the cheerless surroundings of the rather shabby church hall (were there any bright and cheerful buildings in Chasetown, I wondered!), the chairs were arranged for confrontation and it was not difficult—even for an outsider—to identify the two camps. I was glad of the opportunity afforded by that meeting to pick up the vibrations. I made a mental note never to hold any future church council meetings in the church hall. It might be a bit of a squash to fit everyone into the vicarage lounge, but that was where we would meet.

That move in itself changed the whole atmosphere of the meetings. It is much more difficult to make speeches or play to the gallery or lose our tempers in the relaxed atmosphere of a home. People began to listen to one another, rather than take up fixed positions. Argument there most certainly was as we thrashed out basic scriptural principles for key areas of parish life, but there was also a growing respect for different points of view and a desire to find agreement on matters of real importance for the future of the church.

It was clear to me that to introduce a strategy for evangelism in the way we had done at St Thomas' would only exaggerate the divisions within St Anne's. It could only be regarded with suspicion by the long-standing members and pursued eagerly by the newcomers. If it were put to the vote, the church council would be split down the middle, and there would be no clear mandate for it to be introduced. I decided to bide my time until the way ahead became clearer.

Meanwhile, there were plenty of other matters to oocupy my mind: the introduction of the Alternative Service Book and new patterns of Sunday worship, what to do with the church hall, the additional administration that came with being an incumbent, guiding Jonathan through his early months in parish life, trying to get my bearings in a new area, and a million and one other things.

However, I determined that if any opportunities arose to use the outreach course with people I would go ahead on the grounds of pastoral urgency without any formal discussion at the church council. They could hardly object to such a course of action, particularly if it resulted in new people being added to the church. I could also see the advantage of being able to produce living proof of its effectiveness at some later stage when it came to persuading the church council to make it an accepted part of parish policy. It is difficult to argue against something that has already proved its worth.

Opening doors

We had only been in Chasetown a matter of weeks when a

young lady arrived at the vicarage door desperately anxious about her husband, who suffered with severe bouts of depression. Terry was a Christian, Mavoureen a nominal Roman Catholic who clearly needed a living faith to sustain her. Would I come and see her husband? She had come to me because he was Church of England. Of course I would come; but I also talked to her about the benefit of having a team who would come for a number of weeks. They would be able to build a relationship of trust with her husband and help him to find fresh resources in God. Would she mind joining in? She was happy to do so.

Here was our first opportunity. Whom should I send? There wasn't time to explain the course in detail. I needed people who would be able to use the material once and could then themselves lead a team.

The lot fell on Richard, the churchwarden, and Lesley, the wife of the other churchwarden. They formed the first team, with Ann as the leader. Even before the course ended, Mavoureen realised that Jesus was good news for her, not just for her husband, and opened her life to him.

The team was still busy with Terry and Mavoureen when a routine baptism visit turned in an unexpected direction. Melvyn and Carol, like most people who enquire about baptism for their children, had never had more than a fleeting relationship with the church. More honest than some they had decided against a church wedding, not wanting to be hypocrites, as they saw it, by using the church for their own convenience. For the same reason, they had not had their first child, Neil, baptised. Neither had they any intention of seeking baptism for their second child, Emma, when she was born. But matters were taken out of their hands when she was baptised in an emergency in the hospital; it was touch and go whether she would live. In the crisis, Melvyn vowed that if God (about whom he knew next-to-nothing) spared her, he would start to go to church. Emma lived; but, once the crisis was over, Melvyn, like so many who have good intentions, resumed his normal way of life without much thought for God. He did make one visit to church a year or so later, but whatever he was looking for he didn't find it there, nor did his experience encourage him to return. However, God was evidently at work prompting him to enquire about baptism for Neil, seemingly for 'no reason' at all. Quite what put the idea into his head he did not know. After all, Neil was by then five years old, and Emma was two.

None of this was I aware of until we sat chatting in their home about their reasons for wanting Neil baptised. As I was going through the baptism service, explaining what it meant, checking periodically that they understood, Melvyn suddenly asked, 'How can you get Jesus into your life?'

It wasn't the sort of question I had expected him to ask! Where had he picked up such an expression? What did he understand by it? As I pressed him more closely it was obvious that it was a real question springing from a spiritual hunger within. The actual terminology came from a work-mate in the factory who had recently been dramatically converted through the ministry of the local Pentecostal Church. It also became clear that his understanding of what it meant to 'get Jesus into your life' was practically non-existent; and it was even clearer that his wife, Carol, was feeling increasingly uncomfortable with the unexpected turn the conversation had taken. Where were things leading? She only wanted a child baptised!

It was tempting to arrange to see Melvyn on his own and help him to make a personal commitment to Christ, but I resisted—just. 'I could tell you how to get Jesus into your life,' I said, 'but I'm not going to. I think you need to know a bit more about what it might mean before you take that step. I want to suggest that you and Carol have one of our teams from the church to come and discuss it further. Unfortunately, I can't send one immediately, because we have only just started to get the course off the ground and we haven't got many people available. But meanwhile, we'll arrange the baptism for the next family service, and I'll be in touch with you about a team as soon as possible.'

Carol was visibly relieved; Melvyn was willing to be patient; I was trying to contain my excitement.

With no effort on my part, no searching for people willing to receive teams, the Lord had presented us with two openings almost before we had drawn breath.

The new agenda

By the time my first annual church meeting in Chasetown came round, on 31st March 1982, I was in a position to set the direction for the future in the following terms. I feel it is worthwhile to reproduce in full what I said then, as it was the distillation of months of thought and prayer. And while I could not (of course) have known it at the time, these comments were to be the lever God used to challenge the church and open more doors in Chasetown.

'When I came to speak to the PCC last July, before my arrival in the parish, I expressed my conviction that there were many people in this area waiting for the church to take the good news of Jesus Christ to them. My experience in the six months I have been here has confirmed that conviction and impressed on me the urgency to press ahead with evangelism while people are open and responsive. I also spoke of the need to have a good, hard look at ourselves as a church and set ourselves goals and objectives.

'So I turn my attention now to the situation as I see it at present and the way ahead for us as a church in the future.

'If we are to understand our local situation properly, we need to see it against a broader backdrop. We need to see where we are in the whole picture, the place of the Church in society today. That place has changed dramatically since many of you first started going to church, and therefore we need to look afresh at what the church is and must be to minister in a changed and changing society. Unless we see ourselves as we really are, as others see us in society, we cannot hope to put our house in order or plan realistically for the future.

'At this point I want to draw on a leading Roman Catholic theologian, Karl Rahner. In the early 1970s he wrote a little book called *The Shape of the Church to Come*, from which I quote:

> "We cannot for much longer expect the core of practising church people to be surrounded and secured by a large number of those who must still officially be called Christian, giving a false confidence even today when we speak of a Christian society. This

society no longer exists, however fluid the transitions may be between the real Christians and the nominal Christians, however many chances there may be to win back relatively easily such nominal Christians . . . We are a little flock in society and we shall become a much smaller flock, since the erosion of the pre-conditions of a Christian society within the secular society still continues and thus takes away more and more from a traditional Christianity.

"One essential and fundamental consequence of this situation of the church as a dwindling flock is that in her proclamation and in her life she must insist on an aggressive attitude in all situations to win new Christians from an '"unChristian'" milieu and not be content with purely defending her traditional substance . . ."[1]

'I believe that his analysis is absolutely correct. There are still many chances to win back relatively easily nominal Christians, but we need to face the reality that we live in an increasingly secular society, and therefore our strategy as a church cannot be the same as it was when society was largely Christian.

THE TASK

'In the light of that analysis, I see our task as a church in the long term as twofold:
1 To equip ourselves to win back the nominal Christians while there is still time. To make the church grow through evangelism.
2 To structure the life of the Christian fellowship so that we may exist and function more effectively as salt and light in a non-Christian society.

Let me now develop the first of the tasks a little.

'My observation after six months in Chasetown is that there is still a strong residue of nominal, traditional Christianity— but that is dwindling with every generation. I went into a fourth-year class in Chasetown Comprehensive a few weeks ago to answer questions. I was pleased at the sensible and sometimes searching questions these young people were asking about the Christian faith. At the end I asked them how many of them went to church. Not one hand was raised. They do not go because their parents do not go. Traditional Christianity is dying fast.

'So I want to pose two questions to help us focus on the situation as it is here in Chasetown and Chase Terrace.

Why do people stop going to church?
—*physical impossibility* This especially afflicts the very elderly
—*marriage and mobility*
—*other interests* The revolution in travel, holidays, weekends etc
—*the vicar?*

What stops people going back to church?
—*inertia, or habit* Whereas in the past people may have needed a good reason to stop going to church, now they need a good reason to start going.
—*memory* People Jonathan and I meet have often lost contact with the church fifteen or twenty years ago. They remember church as something of an ordeal—formal, impersonal, unwelcoming: a place where you have to be quiet, lose your place in books with small print, listen to meaningless words in archaic language. Sombre, joyless formalism and meaningless ceremonial are what they remember most. They are rather glad to be free of it to enjoy life, and yet many of them are not unsympathetic to what the church stands for, they would almost welcome the opportunity to come back, if they could be sure that it wasn't going to be like it was when they last went. That is why Prayer Book Sung Evensong has no long-term future. When the generation that was brought up on it has gone it will pass into oblivion.

Informality and flexibility are what people respond to today. Have you noticed how informal the royal family has become? How informal our manner of dress has become? Formality imposes a distance between people, it hinders communication. It is appropriate on special occasions but is inappropriate for normal activity.

—*credibility gap* The message we proclaim and the image we project do not tally. That's what people mean when they call church people 'hypocrites'. People look at the building, the sort of worship they remember from the past, the clergy and the people who go to church and say, 'If that's the church, it's not for me.'

How then are we to win these people back? If you haven't read 'Good News Down the Street', may I encourage you to do so? My original title for the booklet was 'Winning Them Back', from a Radio 4 programme of that name which featured the strategy described in the booklet.

'We are planning to launch the scheme in the parish after Easter, and to that end, after consultation with the wardens of both churches, we wish to convene a joint meeting of the two church councils on Wednesday, 21st April to outline and discuss the implications of such a scheme.'

At that meeting I set before people the strategy for outreach which I had described in the Grove Booklet 'Good News Down the Street', published in February that year. At the end of the meeting I took no vote or formal decision, but simply asked those who were willing to be involved in such an undertaking to sign their names on a sheet of paper. Fortunately, I stressed that signing their names did not mean that I would necessarily be able to use them in the immediate future. I say 'fortunately' because when I collected the sheet it had on it forty names from the two congregations!

To say I was taken aback would be an understatement! Where on earth was I going to find all the homes? The thought of starting with thirteen teams was more than a little daunting. But within a matter of weeks thirteen homes had opened up for our teams, and all but one of the people on the list found themselves allocated to teams. The homes were more or less equally divided between the two churches, so Jonathan and his lay people had an early opportunity to try out this approach. On a warm summer's evening in early June we all gathered in the vicarage garden for the one and only briefing they would get before launching out in faith into what was new territory for nearly all of them.

NOTE

1 Karl Rahner, *The Shape of the Church to Come* (SPCK: London, 1974) p31.

CHAPTER THIRTEEN

THE WORD OR THE SPIRIT?

FORTY PEOPLE may have put their names on the list, but not even all of those were convinced that the teams would work. However, as my relationship with the parish was still in the 'honeymoon' phase, they were willing to go along with what I had suggested. Or could it have been that they thought it best to humour the new vicar in the hope that he would come to his senses when the scheme failed?

Funnily enough the loudest mutterings came from the lay readers whom I had helped to train while I was in Aldridge. They were pretty sceptical about the whole idea. Could you really transplant this approach without modification from the middle-class environment for which it had been designed into the working-class culture of Chasetown? It was a question that I, too, was keen to have answered. I could see no reason, in theory, why it shouldn't work equally well with any sort of people, provided they were willing to engage in argument and discussion about the Christian faith. I had already been encouraged by the experience of using the course with Melvyn and Carol, especially since Melvyn had considerable reading problems. I saw them as a sort of firstfruits, a promise of many more to come; but the lay leaders at St John's remained to be convinced. Nor could I blame them. After all, they knew at first hand how different the two parishes were. I could understand their misgivings about its suitability.

Doubting Charlie

It was Charles—or Charlie, as his workmates called him—who expressed that viewpoint most forcefully. He was a shop steward at an engineering firm in Lichfield. Since becoming a Christian he had been deeply involved in evangelistic work among young people in Chase Terrace and was part of a Christian rock group at St John's which ministered not only to youth groups and churches, but also in prisons. He had trained as a lay reader, but his first love was preaching the gospel and seeing others brought to faith in Christ. He wasn't too sure that a University-educated southerner who had no experience of ordinary working life, and who had served in a suburban London parish before coming to middle-class Aldridge, really understood how working people tick. And he was right! The course wasn't designed with such people in mind. Would it really work? The only way to know was to test it.

Charles described his change of mind as follows:

'I admit that I came to the meeting in April holding certain prejudices . . . I regarded St Thomas', Aldridge as a predominantly middle-class church. Already I was dubious that methods of evangelism used in such a situation would be useful to those folks that I wanted to reach for Christ—namely, people who worked on the shop floors of factories such as the one I worked in at that time.

'My burden was to reach the *Sun* readers! How could such a method—so heavily literature-based—reach these people? Perhaps there was in me, too, a resentment of a "whizz-kid" method which appeared to scoff at my own evangelistic attempts.

'However, the meeting was keen to go ahead and so I decided to give it a try. Six teams (from St John's) went out at the same time. I led one of them.

'After two weeks of using the material and seeing its effect on the Coal Board worker (a shop steward like me) and his wife (both divorcees), I was convinced that this method was the greatest thing since sliced bread!

'The material was obviously flexible, well presented (eg a

different colour sheet for each week, page numbers for Bible passages etc) and the conversations were interesting and progressively revealed a greater understanding of the gospel message.

'When these two people committed their lives to Christ, I, together with the two team members, was elated. I needed no more convincing!'

Doubting Michael

In fact, the scheme so caught Charlie's imagination that he began to see possibilities of using it in the factory. It wasn't long before he was badgering me about ways and means of modifying it so that it could be used in that context. It was my turn now to be sceptical! I had never in my wildest moments envisaged it being put to such use, but his enthusiasm was not to be brooked. I was called in to explain the course to the other members of the small Christian fellowship in the factory. They too wanted to try it! I stressed that I really could not help them. I knew nothing about factory life. They would have to use their own initiative and imagination to make it work in that context. Charles describes how they proceeded:

'In my place of work—an engineering firm—we had a small Christian fellowship which met weekly (six members). Although we enjoyed our fellowship and encouraged one another—incidentally, we represented four different denominations—we also wanted to share our faith. Especially, we had opportunities with those who showed an interest in these strange people who gave up their lunch-time once a week to be religious!

'We decided that we would invite the curious to share a "Good News team" in the lunch-time (thirty minutes). Each session would take four lunch breaks per week. We used teams of two members for each "interested enquirer".

'Up to the time I was made redundant (January 1983) we had used three teams to three different people. The results? 1 A lady in her fifties made a commitment to Christ which drew her to a Lichfield church (Anglican), where she is still very active (1987).

2 A Roman Catholic, whose faith came alive in a new way—he is a charismatic Catholic these days!

3 A young man, now married, who, together with his wife, is now a member of St John's Church, Chase Terrace.

'The difficulties of sharing the Good News in such a way are fairly obvious; lost lunch-time, difficulty in finding somewhere to talk quietly, sharing in short bursts, frustration when a crunch point is reached and the work-bell rings! Nevertheless, these shared times show that, given the opportunity, people love to argue, discuss, share, on the subject of who Jesus is.'

Charles has since been ordained into the Church of England and continues to use the material with flair, imagination and enthusiasm—even adapting it to use with twelve- and thirteen-year-olds!

Simplicity—the watchword

The scheme may appear to be heavily dependent on literature and the ability to read—Charles' original misgiving—but the secret of its success under God lies elsewhere. It does not in fact depend on a great deal of reading; even the gospel material contained within the course does not have to be used in its entirety. If it is used woodenly and unimaginatively it will make little impact. And if the sessions are conducted like mini-Bible studies, they will not achieve their purpose.

In fact, the information contained in the biblical material is instead meant to provoke discussion, comment, disagreement, argument—which should be allowed to run freely in any direction. There may sometimes be good reasons for reducing the amount of written material that appears on the sheets. My own inclination would be to use a selection of the passages on the evening, leaving people the option of pursuing the rest on their own if they want to. It is certainly not good policy to make the written content of the course more wide-ranging, however glaring the gaps may be—unless you are working in a highly literate area. Simplicity is essential. Any areas not covered in the written material will certainly be raised by those who have invited the team, and they will raise the issues that are important to them, rather than those that *seem* important to us. The biblical texts provide markers along the way; they point in a certain direction and help to keep people travelling on instead of going round in circles.

Fellow travellers

The team members are not guides, because no two routes on the Christian pilgrimage are identical. They are more like fellow travellers who have discovered that there is an eternal guide. They therefore act as witnesses, bearing testimony to the reality of God, and in so doing are a stimulus and encouragement to others that they too can make that discovery for themselves. They are certainly not 'gurus' or Bible teachers. They simply testify to the genuineness of the Christian message which has taken root in their lives. Real people, for whom God is real, will communicate in any cultural context and across cultures and sub-cultures. If the course were simply an intellectual exercise in pleasant surroundings, its usefulness would be limited to a certain subculture, and its impact would be zero. Of course, care has to be taken to set up a culturally relevant meeting point, but the realm of the Spirit is not confined to the educated middle classes, despite the impression given by many churches, nor do the middle classes have a corner on the ability to communicate spiritual truth by word of mouth. The Acts of the Apostles should have taught us that: 'The members of the Council were amazed to see how bold Peter and John were and to learn that they were ordinary men of no education. They realised then that they had been companions of Jesus' (Acts 4:13).

The key to the success of the scheme among ordinary working people is that they are just as able to discern spiritual reality and respond to it as anyone else. Word of mouth, backed up by the presence of Jesus in people's lives by his Spirit, has the same power to communicate today as it had in the first or any other century. Spiritual need is not confined to any one section of the community, and more people than we always realise are looking for a satisfying meaning to their lives.

JOHN AND MONA

John had sung in a church choir as a lad. A solo that he had sung at the funeral of a young Cub had made a deep impression on him. Like so many, however, he left that all behind as he grew up and began his working life. But I'll let him tell his own story . . .

'In 1975 I was overworking and suffered a mental breakdown, but in all the time I was ill I never forgot that somehow He was still with me. But when I was discharged I did not do what I was told. I carried on chasing money, the worst thing I have ever done. Now I was on big money I wanted more work—sometimes seven twelve-hour night shifts. I always stayed on nights because I could also work after a few hours' sleep during the day. Well, I thought I could.

'One night I was working at two hundred feet above the ground, up in the boilers of the power station. Suddenly I stopped. The rest of the men looked at me and asked if I was all right. I did not answer. I just stood up amid the thick dust and found a ladder to the ground. I walked to the cabin, took off my boilersuit and boots. Somehow, although I did not know what I was doing, I managed to find my way home. I did not know it then, but I was in a worse state than when I was released from St George's Hospital in Stafford seven years previously. I was admitted to St Matthew's Hospital in May 1982, where it was discovered that I had a lack of lithium in my blood and would have to take drugs for the rest of my life.

'Again I worked hard to try and give my wife and family a better way of life. I was taking a lot of drugs—about thirty-five a day, if I remember rightly. My marriage broke up and I was left with nothing. My home was a dirty flat in Chasetown.'

John was then befriended by Mona, who was later to become his wife. She took him home and cared for him in his befuddled state until . . .

'One Friday morning, at about six o'clock, I heard something I had not heard for nearly fourteen years: the birds singing outside my bedroom window. At that precise moment I knew the Lord had called me. I got out of bed, dressed, went into the lounge and opened the curtains. I cannot explain the joy I felt . . . tears came rolling down my face uncontrollably. I have felt a lot of things in my life, but never had I felt anything like that.

'On Sunday I got ready, not for work, but at long last to sing praises to the Lord.'

John came to St Anne's that morning with a somewhat reluctant Mona in tow. In September 1985 he and Mona did the outreach course together and were confirmed in the November. They have never looked back and talk freely and unashamedly about the difference Jesus has made to their lives, an impact that is evident to others, despite their sometimes stormy relationship and the complicated domestic situation around them.

ADRIAN

One of those who was intrigued, not only by their Jesus talk, but also by the fact that they enjoyed going to church, was Adrian. He lived on the same council estate and had known Mona for several years. A young man of thirty, he had been unemployed for a number of years after an accident at work which left him unable to walk without sticks. I first met Adrian at the church barn dance in the Roman Catholic school. Of course, it was John and Mona who had persuaded him to come. He thoroughly enjoyed himself—and joined in the dances, complete with sticks! That evening's fun overcame all his misgivings about church people, and on Sunday morning he was at St Anne's with John and Mona. When Confirmation was mentioned in the notices some weeks later, he was the first to put his name down.

It was only then that I discovered that he couldn't read and write very well. He was worried that he might not be able to do the course. I soon reassured him on that point. I explained to him that, as the outreach course was the basis of our Confirmation preparation, there would be no problems. He wouldn't have to read anything; the team members could do all the reading that was required. As with many people who could not read, Adrian relied on his memory. His powers of retention were highly developed, and by the end of the course he knew more of the New Testament by heart than the team members!

Adrian wasn't the first person with reading difficulties to do the course. Melvyn, our firstfruits, had not only discovered new life in Christ, but also a desire to read that enabled him to overcome the problems. And just the previous year another couple on the estate, living not far from Adrian, had become Christians using the course, despite the wife's reading problems. So selecting a team for Adrian was easy. Melvyn's personal understanding of what it feels like and his testimony to the way the Lord had helped him with his own reading difficulties has proved enormously valuable in such situations. Needless to say, Adrian now rejoices in his new-found faith and spends hours reading painstakingly through his Bible. He told me soon afterwards how much he was looking forward to Christmas. It would be the first time he had ever been to church on Christmas Day.

The witness of people such as these has led to others on the estate becoming aware of the good news and its relevance to ordinary people's lives, so that we are seeing the beginnings of an effective Christian presence in an area of the parish largely untouched by the church. It is a close-knit community, many of whom were born and bred in Chasetown. The network of relationships is such that one or two people becoming Christians heightens the awareness of many more that the church (for it is in those terms that people think) may be relevant to them.

THE ALLPORTS

The Allport family was a case in point. It was Melvyn's wife,

Carol, who was the all-important link with them. As a child she had lived in the same street as they had and gone to school with their daughter, Carollyn. She had always kept in touch with them and they knew that she had started going to church at St Anne's.

When she called round one evening just before Christmas 1985, the mother mentioned wistfully that she had been wanting to go to church herself for some time but had never done anything aout it. Her next door neighbour, Kath, had invited her to go with her more than once, but she had never taken up the offer. Carol suggested that it might be a good idea to have a chat with the vicar first. Should she ask him to call? Hilary, the mother, was non-committal, but as Carol left, the son, Stephen, a single man in his late twenties, caught her at the door and urged her to ask me to call. She wasted no time in doing so, calling at the vicarage on the way home!

When I came the next day, it was clear that Stephen as well as his mother were spiritually open. She had been unwell for some time and was waiting to go into hospital. Stephen's job as a waiter with its unsocial hours did not bring him a great deal of fulfilment. I talked to them about the outreach course as a way into the church. It would mean that Stephen could be involved, even though he was nearly always working on Sunday mornings. They were definitely interested. But what about Hilary's husband, Dennis? They thought it very unlikely he would join in—and they proved to be right! Whenever the team came, Dennis was down at his 'local'. However, by dint of a few delaying tactics, the team managed still to be around when he returned home, so at least he got to know them.

What I hadn't realised when Carol asked me to call about a team was that the daughter, Carollyn, and her husband, Ron, also lived in the same house. Ron, who has considerable hearing difficulties, worked in a warehouse, while Carollyn worked in a factory. Would they be interested in joining in? They were clearly much more reluctant and suspicious than Hilary and Stephen, but they eventually agreed.

We were all set to begin early in January 1986. Then

Hilary's hospital appointment came through, and the course had to be postponed. It wasn't until after Easter that we finally managed to begin. The outcome was that all four made a commitment to Christ and started to come to St Anne's. For six weeks Dennis faithfully drove them to church each Sunday morning and collected them afterwards. Then Carollyn reminded him of an earlier conversation when she had asked him point blank when he was going to start going to church.

'I'll go when you go,' he had replied. There was no way he could wriggle out, so taking his courage in both hands, he crossed the threshold the following Sunday morning. Two years later he is still coming faithfully and isn't far from the kingdom.

Here is a perfect example of how the gospel can sometimes spread through the natural network of relationships within a community.

The parable of the Sower

The question of whether the course would work in a working-class culture has largely been answered in my own mind. My experience in Chasetown encourages me to think that it is not so much cultural factors as spiritual openness that dictates whether it will work or not.

A comparison of the figures for the equivalent six-year period at St Thomas' and St Anne's (ie the first six years of its use in each church) reveals that a higher percentage of people have been converted in Chasetown from a similar number of opportunities, with a higher number also going on to become disciples. (It is a little early to assess 1987 and 1988, so those figures are not included.) I have shown years 1 and 2 in the same column simply because in both churches we launched the course in the autumn and the number of teams operating in the first year was very small. The figures from both churches show clearly that there can be a considerable variation in the number of opportunities from year to year. The fact that the number of teams sent out by St Thomas' decreases in each year in this sample is of no

St Thomas', Aldridge (1974–1979) compared with St Anne's, Chasetown (1981–1986)

Year	Number of teams sent out	Number of people receiving a team	Number of commitments	Percentage of commitments	Number of disciples	Percentage of disciples
1/2	24 (11)†	42* (21*)	22 (15)	67% (83%)	17 (11)	52% (61%)
3	14 (9)	26* (15)	16 (13)	70% (87%)	15 (11)	65% (73%)
4	11 (17)	21* (26*)	13 (20)	65% (95%)	11 (13)	55% (62%)
5	10 (5)	20* (9)	12 (8)	71% (89%)	12 (8)	71% (89%)
6	7 (19)	13* (37*)	11 (26)	92% (74%)	7 (22)	58% (62%)
Total	66 (61)	122 (108)	74 (82)	70% (84%)	62 (65)	59% (66%)

†The figures for St Anne's are given in brackets.

* Included in this total are some who were already disciples, usually married to non-Christian spouses. They have been included in this total in order to give an accurate picture of the total number of people who have done the course. However, in calculating the percentages they have been omitted so as not to distort the true impact the course has made.

significance. In year 7 they sent out 18 teams and in year 8 they needed 36! I could not continue the comparison between the two churches beyond year 6 as detailed figures were not available. However, the important points emerge from the more limited sample. It is noticeable that there is also considerable fluctuation in the degree of success achieved from year to year. Again I would hesitate to read any great significance into the fluctuations. I am sure they had nothing to do with the calibre of the teams we sent out or the quality of 'after care' that people received. It is simply that the level of response will inevitably vary from person to person. If they do anything it is perhaps to remind us not to become over-confident when we have a good year nor to be too discouraged when we have a lean year.

However thorough may be our preparation, however skilful our harvesting, however all-embracing our nurture of new converts, the seed of the gospel will be received with varying degrees of commitment, and only some of it will bear lasting fruit in terms of a life of discipleship.

CHAPTER FOURTEEN

SNAPSHOTS

I N THE PRECEDING CHAPTERS I have used a combination of real-life examples and statistics to try and convey the impact our outreach strategy has had on the two parishes in which I have been personally involved. The examples I have used have, naturally, been selected to illustrate different aspects of the course and the way it works. The process of selection has been inevitably somewhat arbitrary. I have written about those situations that sprang to mind, which means those that were the most striking or interesting to me. The result is that the ordinary and the unsuccessful have not featured largely in these pages; nor has there been much discussion about the problems or difficulties we encountered.

What I have written may therefore sound too good to be true. Surely there must be some snags?! Of course there are. The reason they have not been given much space is not a desire to give the impression of unmitigated success, but simply because they have never loomed large in our thinking. That is not to say that we shut our eyes to the potential problems, or the actual ones; rather we took the view that we should expect there to be snags and difficulties—we should not expect everything to go smoothly—but we determined not to be deterred by them, nor to spend time worrying about them in advance. If we spend time concentrating on all the possible snags that can arise (and our minds are amazingly fertile!), a deadly paralysis can easily set in.

We decided to deal with the problems when they arose and not before, and to trust God to give us the strength and the wisdom there and then. Prayer and common sense seem to be perfectly adequate in most situations. I cannot remember when I was last approached by a team leader with a problem that required more than that.

It would be possible (and for some, no doubt, the temptation would be irresistible) to spend a lot of time training church members in problem-solving techniques,. and, no doubt, they would feel better for it; but they might not then feel quite the same need to rely on the Holy Spirit. In our experience honest mistakes and the expression of ignorance on the part of team members have never been a stumbling block in sharing the good news of Jesus Christ. Of course, if people already have skills and knowledge they can be a great asset on a team in certain situations. I am certainly not advocating ignorance as a virtue, but a loving, caring attitude and a desire to find out, more than compensates for lack of knowledge or skill with words.

I have therefore been loath to spend time in these pages offering solutions to problems that we have encountered. For one thing I have never kept any record of specific problems that have arisen and how they were dealt with; for another, I do not believe we have anything to share that would not be better learned by others 'on the job'.

The other drawback in selecting examples to illustrate my point is that it does not convey an accurate impression of what a period of concentrated outreach involves in terms of the variety of situations that may be encountered. Still, I hope I may be able to remedy both these deficiencies by presenting a series of 'portraits' from the current outreach programme at St Anne's (January–April 1988) which involved sixteen teams—the largest number we have yet had to field at one time. Such a large sample should provide a reasonable cross-section of situations, problems that arise, and the immediate outcome of the teams' activities.

The first impact of such a large number of teams—involving 47 different church members (one third of the regular congregation)—is on the normal midweek activities.

By the end of November 1987 I was in a position to alert house group leaders that all of the groups would be affected to a greater or lesser degree in January or February by calls on their members to join teams. In the event one group had to close down completely as all its members were required. We were hard pressed to find sufficient team leaders to match the demand. One of the church wardens ended up leading two separate teams, the first on a Tuesday afternoon, the second on a Wednesday evening. I hasten to add that he did volunteer!

The information for the following snapshots has come from those doing the course as well as from the team members, enabling me to report the situations, I hope, with some degree of accuracy. I trust they will be enlightening. Many of them came as the result of visits by one lay person, Margaret, who went to nearly fifty homes over a period of weeks following up a routine post-baptismal letter. There is no significance in the order in which they come.

Ewart and Lynda, a young couple in their late twenties, moved to Chasetown five years ago from the neighbouring parish of Brownhills, where their first child, Jamie, was baptised shortly before they left. In June 1986, Vicki was born and the following January they made an approach about baptism for her. When I visited the home to discuss it with them I discovered that Lynda had gone to Sunday school. Although her active contact with the church had long since lapsed, she was quite open and well disposed to the suggestion of coming to our monthly family service. Ewart was not over enthusiastic about the idea. After all, he worked six days a week as a brake press operator. He had never had any contact with the church. He had not been baptised, nor had he gone to Sunday school. The prospect of attending a normal church service once a month did not sound like good news to him, but, as I pointed out, the baptism service required them to give an undertaking that they would give their children a Christian upbringing within the family of the church, and, I assured him, he would probably enjoy the family service with its informal, relaxed atmosphere.

When I asked about their choice of god-parents I was surprised and delighted to hear them mention Jackie, one of our church members who lived just along the road. It transpired that she had befriended Lynda when they first moved to Chasetown. They had met at the bus stop as Lynda was struggling with a pushchair and a young baby and discovered that they lived in the same road. Lynda was very shy, but Jackie's warm, outgoing personality and her gentle friendliness gradually won her confidence. She was an obvious choice to be one of the god-parents to Vicki. The baptism, in the context of the Mothering Sunday family service, was a joyfully chaotic affair. Ewart found that the church was not quite what he had anticipated, and Lynda was surprised to see others there whom she recognised. They began to appear regularly once a month despite the distractions created by an energetic four-year-old and a baby, and even if they sometimes spent as much time in the creche as in the service!

In the late autumn of 1987 Ewart and Lynda were sent the following routine letter:

Dear Ewart & Lynda,

When you had Vicki baptised you undertook to give her a Christian upbringing within the family of the church until such time as she is old enough to come to confirmation.

I am writing to you because I see from your baptism application that you yourselves have not been confirmed. It may therefore be difficult for you to encourage your child to be confirmed when the time comes.

I shall be starting a six-week course—for adults only—in January 1988. It can take place in your own home, so that you do not have to worry about finding baby-sitters. It consists of a series of informal discussions about the Christian faith, which would give you a better understanding of what Christians believe and help you to give your child the Christian upbringing you promised.

Whether or not you wish to be confirmed at the end of the course you would certainly be in a better position to help your child live the Christian life.

A member of the congregation will be calling on you in the next few weeks to explain how it works and to enquire whether you wish to take part.

Yours sincerely,

Michael Wooderson

Margaret called a few days later. Ewart was out, but Lynda expressed a keen interest in the course. She wasn't sure about Ewart, but Margaret put him down anyway—after all he couldn't easily avoid joining in if it was taking place all around him! Fortunately he didn't raise too many objections to this *fait accompli*.

When it came to selecting a team, Jackie was an obvious choice. She was delighted to have the opportunity, only having been on one team four years previously. Jenny, a young mother with two children, joined her. She had become a Christian at the end of 1985 as a result of the course and had just one opportunity to be on a team since then. I needed a man to complete the team, and it clearly needed to be someone who had the experience to lead. Pete agreed to head it, even though he was not completely fit.

In the event, Pete was unable to be present at three out of the six sessions, and on one occasion had to cry off at the very last minute. Despite their inexperience Jenny and Jackie did a marvellous job of completing the course and had the great thrill of leading Ewart and Lynda in a prayer of commitment. When I called round to see Jenny just before the final session to brief her about how to handle the commitment section and the best point at which to use the video of *Journey into Life*, I left with *her* reassuring *me* not to worry! She had every confidence that the Lord would take charge.

This situation admirably illustrates the value of having three members in a team. Without that provision it would not have been possible to complete the course with Ewart and Lynda. Of course, it is not often that teams are affected to quite the same degree by the leader being ill, but it does show that two pretty inexperienced church members can carry on successfully when they are unexpectedly thrown in at the deep end.

However, those were not the only disruptions the team

had to cope with. They had to conduct the course with both children present—and active!—until they fell asleep (the children, that is, not the team members!). Clearly they could not wait until the children were asleep before they started, so they had to carry on regardless. It goes without saying that it is not easy to concentrate or hold an uninterrupted discussion in such circumstances, but it did not prevent Ewart and Lynda from hearing and understanding enough about Jesus to want to follow him.

When Vicki, the eighteen-month-old, was rushed into hospital with suspected meningitis, it looked as though the course might be delayed indefinitely. Fortunately, it was a false alarm and she was only detained two days; by the following week she was well enough for the course to be able to resume.

Despite all the difficulties Ewart and Lynda both came to faith and are going on strongly with the Lord. They were confirmed together in May 1988 and rarely miss a Sunday.

Andrew and Sharon, another young couple in their late twenties, set up home in Chasetown in 1983. Sharon came from Coalpool, near Walsall, where she attended a Methodist Sunday School for a few years before losing interest. Andrew's home was Aldridge, where he also attended the Methodist Sunday School until he was fourteen.

It was only when they were thinking about marriage that they renewed their contact with the church. They began to attend Aldridge Parish Church—Sharon more often than Andrew, it has to be said—together with Andrew's parents who themselves started to go to church after a long absence. When they moved to Chasetown, it was a couple of years before Sharon made contact with St Anne's. It was the birth of Adam in 1986 that prompted her to come. The request for baptism gave me an opportunity to talk with them in some depth and encourage them to attend the monthly family service.

Andrew rarely, if ever, appeared, but Sharon began to come occasionally and then more regularly as her interest quickened. Some months after the baptism I broached with them the matter of an outreach team coming to their home. Sharon was interested, but Andrew was clearly not well disposed towards the idea, so I did not press the question further. At the end of 1987 Sharon, who had been coming to St Anne's quite regularly for a while, expressed an interest in being confirmed. I explained to her that the course would take place in her own home, and it would be nice if Andrew could be persuaded to join in. This time he was happy to do so.

For a long time he had been wanting to join the police force, and at last the opportunity had arisen. Of course, that entailed selling their house and moving out of Chasetown. How long that would take we did not know, so we started the course not knowing whether we would be able to complete it. After the initial apprehension of the first week, when the television was left on as background, Andrew got more and more involved as the course progressed and confessed afterwards to having thoroughly enjoyed the team's visits. Although he did not reach the point of making a commitment to Christ at the end of the course, his understanding and appreciation of the Christian faith had progressed to the stage where he was aware of what such a step involved.

At the end of March 1988 they moved to Cannock, just five miles away, so it is still possible to keep in touch with them. Sharon was confirmed in May that year and continues to grow in her new-found faith. She has been able to attend a nurture group and comes to church most Sundays. Our contact with Andrew will obviously be scarce, and we must trust that the Lord will speak to him through Sharon and through other Christians with whom he comes into touch.

We first met Harold and Brenda when they came to the Christmas Eve Communion in 1987. They were both born and bred in the locality and had attended Sunday School in their younger days, then dropping out in their teens. When she left school, Brenda went to work at the vicarage in Burntwood, started to go to church and was duly confirmed. It was at Burntwood Church that she first met Harold, who sang in the choir. They were married at St Anne's in 1950 and from then on they attended church only rarely.

Harold's job as a baker/confectioner came to a premature end two years ago when it was discovered that he had heart trouble. With time on his hands, he began to reflect on life and its meaning. In November 1987 the parish magazine carried an announcement about the forthcoming confirmation preparation course for adults. He had never been confirmed, so it seemed a good opportunity to sort out the questions that were going round in his mind. So it was that as they left church on Christmas Eve, Harold asked if he could be prepared for confirmation.

When John, Hilary and Edna went to do the course with them they were warmly received and built up good relations with Harold and Brenda. There were no problems, and at the end both of them were happy to pray the prayer of commitment. However, when it came to the further commitment of confirmation and church membership, Harold did not feel ready to move ahead. They were under pressure at that time domestically, and I tried to reassure them that they shouldn't feel guilty about marking time for a while.

Sadly, we have rarely seen them since and only time will tell whether they eventually come into the full life of the fellowship. Meanwhile, we continue to pray for them and visit on a casual basis.

Our first contact with Maurice and Yvonne came in October 1987. Phyllis, who lives on the same council estate and only started coming to St Anne's six months before, was delivering the parish magazine and got into conversation with Yvonne. As she talked about St Anne's Yvonne expressed the desire to get involved—she had gone to Sunday school at St Anne's from the age of five until she left school at fifteen, but, apart from her wedding in 1968 and the baptism of the children, she had never been back. She had lived in Chasetown since the age of three and moved into the house next door when she got married. Phyllis alerted me to the opportunity, and I called round without delay. There I met the rest of the family: Maurice, a miner in his early forties, out of work for the past three years, admitted that he once went to Sunday School—but only for about six months.

Maurice had joined the army at sixteen and served for six and a half years, during which time he married Yvonne and the first two children were born, Anthony now nineteen and Helen now eighteen. Anthony was born with a mental handicap, albeit not a severe one, but when Helen was born with the same handicap, Maurice had little choice but to leave the army to give Yvonne the support she needed. While he was in the army, Maurice went through Confirmation instruction and was confirmed.

He found work as a miner in one of the local pits until he was made redundant in 1985. Their family was completed by Kevin, now fifteen, who shares the same handicap as his brother and sister. With their hands full in this way, it is not really surprising that Maurice and Yvonne had little time to devote to anything outside the home.

However, for a while before her encounter with Phyllis, Yvonne had experienced a growing longing to come back to church. Kevin always enjoyed watching *Songs of Praise* on the television, and Yvonne had promised to take him to the 'real thing' one day—but it is not easy to take such a step, especially with the anxiety about whether Kevin would behave himself. What sort of reception would she get? Would she have the embarrassment of Kevin creating a disturbance? Would people understand?

I was able to set her mind at rest on that score and to encourage her that there would be people at church whom she already knew so that she would quickly feel at home. The following Sunday she was there with Helen and Kevin and has hardly missed a Sunday since. She cannot always bring Kevin because he is such a handful, but invariably Helen comes with her, and on Mothering Sunday the whole family was present for the first time.

If the family's first step towards faith came when Yvonne brought Helen and Kevin to church at the end of October, the next step came with the visit of the evangelist, Ian Knox, to preach at a special carol service two weeks before Christmas. Among the thirty or so people who came forward in response to his appeal for commitment (about a quarter of the congregation!) were Helen and Yvonne.

Yvonne had already indicated an interest in being confirmed, so the next thing was to persuade Maurice to join in the course when it began in January. He was happy to do so. The best time, probably the only time, a team could go would be while the three children were at school. Roy, one of the churchwardens, who had taken early retirement, and his wife Noreen were obvious candidates and keen to go; John, who was unemployed and lived on the same estate, made up the threesome. Maurice didn't say a lot as the course proceeded, but he had no hesitation in praying the prayer of commitment. It will clearly not be easy to integrate the whole family fully into the life of the church, but the first stage has been negotiated smoothly.

Ellen lives on the council estate with her husband, Dave, and her two children, Hayley aged ten and Matthew aged eight. Dave is a foreman at an engineering firm in Lichfield, where they first met. Ellen comes from a mining family and lived in the north east of England until she was eleven, when the family moved to the Midlands to find work. Dave and Ellen moved to Chasetown from Lichfield in 1978 when Hayley was just six weeks old. Two years later Matthew was born. Like Maurice and Yvonne's children, he suffers from a mental handicap, but he does attend church with his mother from time to time.

Ellen's first real contact with St Anne's came through Val, one of our church members, who worked as a playground helper at Hayley's school. Val helps to run the nine-to-eleven-year-olds' Pathfinder Group at St Anne's and spotted Hayley as a potential member. She joined the group in 1987 after a visit from Val, who then befriended Ellen and took her along to our Wednesday afternoon 'Open Doors' meeting. Ellen also began to attend the monthly family service with Hayley and Matthew. Her contact with other Christians in church and on Wednesday afternoons aroused a spiritual hunger within her. 'I felt they had something I didn't,' she confessed. The discussions on Christian faith and life at 'Open Doors', earthed in the experience of many there who had recently become Christians, led her to a point of commitment one Wednesday in the autumn of 1987.

When people become Christians in this way it is always our policy still to take them through the outreach course to make sure that we build a sure foundation for their future growth. We would have liked to involve Dave, but the time was not right, and a team of three, including two from the council estate, worked through the course with Ellen in the daytime while the children were at school. She was also confirmed in May 1988 and continues to grow in the faith, showing her love for God in many practical ways in the community.

John and Anne, a couple in their early forties, with two grown up children, had moved to Chasetown from Birmingham twenty-one years ago, but had never made any real contact with St Anne's apart from having their children baptised. However, in August 1987 Anne attended a wedding at the church and asked the verger afterwards what time the Sunday service was. Whenever the thought had crossed her mind before to start going to church, she had made the excuse to herself that she didn't know the times of the services. Now she did know; but it was still a few weeks before she plucked up the courage to come.

It wasn't at all what she expected. Everyone was so friendly. She came for three weeks on her own. The fourth week John came with her. It was a fortnight before Christmas, and we had an evangelistic carol service with the Church Pastoral-Aid Society evangelist, Ian Knox. When he invited people to come to the front, John had gone almost before Anne realised it. She hastily joined him at the front, and together they opened their lives to God.

Like Ellen, they too went through the outreach course to give them a good grounding. It took twice as long in their case, not because they were slow learners, but because John's shifts meant that they could only meet fortnightly. They were confirmed together in May, 1988.

Tracey was another person who went forward on that occasion in December. She had already expressed a desire to be confirmed and was in line to receive a team with her fiancé,

Grahame. He had absolutely no church background but was willing to join in to please Tracey. Earlier experiences with the Jehovah's Witnesses who lived next door had put him off religion completely. He was quite adamant that he didn't believe in God, but he was open to engage in an honest discussion.

The team had to face some straight and searching questions. Grahame tended to make most of the running. Both of them genuinely enjoyed those evenings, and when the course finished Grahame was keen to join Tracey in the Welcome group and the Confirmation course, even though he had not reached a point where he felt able to make a decision for Christ. Of course, we were only too pleased to oblige, and the promise of continued contact with him may well bear fruit in the not too distant future. He was present at Tracey's Confirmation in May, which made a considerable impact on him.

Grace, a bubbly fifty-year-old housewife with two grown up sons and a boy of nine, first made contact in 1986 when Roy, who was then seven, began to ask her about baptism. She had gone to church with her mother years before, but it was a fairly nominal and occasional activity. When I discussed Roy's baptism with her and her husband, I impressed on them the importance of coming to church as a family and the need for Roy to belong to the Sunday school.

She took both those matters seriously and began to appear regularly at family services. Her interest grew until at the end of 1987 she inquired about being confirmed. Her husband was happy for her to go ahead with the course, although he himself did not wish to join in. So a team of three ladies took her through it in the afternoons. She was quite fearful at first that it might be too studious but soon relaxed and enjoyed it immensely. The only difficulty the team encountered was her tendency to accept everything that was said without much question. This makes it very hard for the team members to assess how much is really sinking in, and in some situations it can be quite demoralising. In this case they need not have worried for Grace was ready to follow Christ, and the commitment prayer meant a great deal to her. She, too, was confirmed in May 1988 and goes on her way rejoicing.

John and Christine   received our routine letter to parents who had recently had a child baptised and responded positively. A couple in their early thirties, they had moved to Chasetown in 1986, and baby Helen was born in October of that year. John is an electrical engineer, Christine a biology teacher. They met while at university in Nottingham through a mutual interest in bell-ringing, an interest which they keep up at St Luke's, Cannock. (We have no bells in Chasetown!)

John's parents were churchgoers, and he had attended Sunday school regularly as a child, only to drop out during his teens. However, his interest was revived at university, and he was confirmed during that time. Christine meanwhile had not been confirmed, hence her interest in the course. It was clear as the discussions proceeded that they both had a Christian faith but did not find involvement in the local church easy. Christine did not in fact proceed to Confirmation, and further contact with them may be limited.

David and Heather   also received the letter inviting them to do the course, and when Margaret called to see them she discovered that they were only too willing to take part. Heather has been connected with St Anne's all her life; her mother was a faithful and prayerful member of the church until her death in January 1987. Heather came up through the Sunday school and attended church regularly, if not each week. David's connections were more with St John's, as he lived in Chase Terrace, but they didn't really extend beyond his Sunday school days.

They were married at St Anne's in February 1982 and set up home in Chase Terrace. Miles was born a year later and baptised soon after. But it was only after the birth of Vida in May 1986 that Heather began to feel that her Christian faith was inadequate. She had been searching for a couple of years when the offer of a team presented her with an opportunity to explore these matters more fully. David was very happy to join in, though before the team came they did both wonder what they were letting themselves in for! But Roy, Margaret and Marjorie soon put them at ease.

As the weeks went by David became increasingly interested, while Heather was helped to sort out a number of misunderstandings about the Christian faith that were a stumbling block to her making a full commitment to Christ. She and David both opened their hearts to God at the end of the course and David went on to be confirmed in May 1988—Heather had already been confirmed as a teenager.

When Barry and Mary approached me　about being married at St Anne's, they were uncertain whether it would be possible as Mary had been divorced. Both of them came from the council estate, and both of them had attended Sunday school at St Anne's as youngsters—although Barry dropped out rather sooner than Mary. She continued to attend church until she got married at the age of eighteen in 1974. She moved first to Rugeley, then to Lichfield, never more than five or six miles from Chasetown.

Darren was born in 1975, followed by Susannah in 1978. By 1982 the marriage had broken down and Mary moved back to Chasetown with the children and lived with her mother. She picked up her links with the church again, coming regularly to the monthly family service with the children when Susannah started at Sunday school.

In September 1987 she met Barry, a single man of her own age, and he began to appear at church with her. It was towards the end of the year when they broached the subject of marriage with me. I explained that the church council had set down certain preconditions for the marriage of divorced persons, which would require them to worship at St Anne's regularly for at least six months and go through a course about the Christian faith. They were happy to comply with those requirements, and I made arrangements for a team to work with them.

As neither of them had a home base which we could use I arranged for them to go to the home of one of our church families, Tony and Mary, who would do the course with them. They had some lively and worthwhile discussions which moved them on in their understanding of the Christian faith, although the course ended inconclusively. The relationships they have built up with the church are strong. They will be living locally, which will enable us to continue our links with them.

Robin and Kerrie first came in contact with St Anne's through a baptism enquiry. A young couple in their early twenties, they had moved from Aldridge to Chasetown after their marriage in September 1983. They had both had some connection with Sunday school in their younger days, and Robin had attended the Church of England Primary School in Aldridge, but beyond that their involvement with the church was non-existent.

When I visited them about the baptism of their daughter Hayley, I was impressed by their friendliness and openness. Hayley was baptised in June 1986, but there was no further contact with the church afterwards. However, when Margaret followed up our routine letter in the autumn of 1987, they agreed to invite a team to do the course with them. They could only meet fortnightly because of Robin's shifts, and this did affect the continuity.

They began on 14th January and didn't finish until 28th March, which certainly made it harder to maintain the momentum. Despite these difficulties the team made good progress, and Robin and Kerrie appreciated all that they learnt even though at the end they were not ready to make a commitment to Christ. Sue, the team leader, lives just up the road from them and is in regular contact with them, so there will be further opportunities to share the good news with them.

Lee and Jayne If the team that went to Robin and Kerrie found the lack of continuity difficult, that was nothing compared with the problems encountered by Bill, Val and Debbie when they went to Lee and Jayne, a young couple in their twenties. Again, the original point of contact was an enquiry about baptism. Jayne had no church background, and although Lee had been involved with a Pentecostal church in his teens, he had not continued the link. They were married at Brownhills Parish Church (the next door parish to Chasetown) in 1983 and moved to Chasetown in 1985.

In February 1986 Leanne was born. She was baptised at St Anne's later that year. There was no further contact with the church until we followed up the baptism in the autumn of 1987, when Lee and Jayne agreed to invite a team into their home. The course was dogged with unexpected complications. Week one had to be called off because Lee and Jayne were ill. The following week when the team arrived Jayne's parents were there and it was impossible to do anything. At the third attempt they managed to make a start and decided to catch up on lost time by combining sessions one and two. It was just as well they had, because the following week the baby went down with measles, and they had to cancel again. A week later they had the all clear and managed to complete session three.

When the team arrived the week afterwards, they discovered that Lee had changed his job and was now working shifts, so they were thwarted yet again. From now on they could only meet once a fortnight. They did complete session four the following week and a fortnight later, with time running out, they did sessions five and six on consecutive evenings. Needless to say the outcome was not positive, but Lee and Jayne enjoyed what they learnt, and Val has been keeping in touch.

Laurence and Ann   When Margaret returned from another of her follow-up visits after our routine letter to say that Laurence and Ann would do the course, I knew it would not be easy to find the right team because of Laurence's job. Long-distance lorry drivers tend to have an erratic and unpredictable home life. In fact, the only evening he could guarantee being at home on a regular basis was on a Sunday. I have always avoided sending teams out at the weekend for the sake of everyone concerned, but clearly in this case I had no choice.

Whom could I send? The one person who immediately

sprang to mind was Melvyn. Because he is a shift worker it is not always easy to fit him into a team, but if he was available he would actually be able to be present at every session—a new experience for him! I was confident that he would relate easily to Laurence. I only discovered later that they had been at school together, though neither of them were local people!

Rita and Yvonne completed the team. Both of them have only been Christians for a year or so and are full of fun and enthusiasm. I knew they would befriend Ann as they only lived along the road. They are both in their fifties, and Yvonne has grandchildren of her own, so it seemed a good combination. Once the course began, it ran without a hitch. The team built good relationships with Laurence and Ann, who were interested to learn. They considered themselves to be Christians already, although they rarely went to church. As the course unfolded, they found that there was a lot more to being a Christian than they had appreciated, but they didn't get as far as making a commitment. They needed more time to assimilate what they had learned before making a decision. However, the prospects for continuing contact with them are good. In May 1988, as I write, Ann has just had a baby boy to add to their eighteen-month-old daughter, Rachel.

Melvyn and Elaine, a young couple in their twenties, whom I had married at St Anne's in October, 1985 presented a different set of practical problems. When their first daughter Katie was baptised in October 1986, I discovered that Elaine had quite a strong church background and a desire to renew those links. However, Melvyn had no such background and led such a busy life as a motor technician that it was impossible to consider sending a team to them at that stage. By the time they enquired about baptism for the next child, Amie, a year later, they had moved house within the area, and Melvyn had changed his job to an even more demanding one.

The previous year Elaine had expressed an interest in being confirmed, but the time was not right. This time when I called she was much more positive, and so was Melvyn.

Elaine was suffering with post-natal depression, and it was clear that Melvyn was very concerned about her and the children. As a works supervisor at Land Rover he had to leave for work at 7 a.m. and was often not home until 7 p.m. He was then so tired that he didn't have much energy left for Elaine and two demanding children.

The only evening on which we could do the course with them was Melvyn's day off, which changed by one day each week. We needed a team who could be available on any day of the week, a man who would be able to relate to Melvyn, and two ladies who could befriend and support Elaine in practical as well as prayerful ways. I wondered where I would find such people among our busy congregation, but Dave, Hazel and Joan came up trumps. They surrounded Elaine with the gentle love, support and encouragement she needed. They acted as baby-sitters, so that Melvyn and Elaine could have time together. In every way they sought to show practical Christian love. The result was that Melvyn and Elaine made a commitment to Christ together. Elaine was confirmed at a memorable service in May 1988, and they are both continuing to grow in the faith. The relationships they forged with the team members are also continuing as their practical love makes it possible for Elaine and Melvyn to attend the Welcome group together as well as find space for each other on other occasions.

June and Carol Two housewives from the council estate complete the picture. We first made contact with June through the baptism of her fourth child in August 1986. She knew a number of the women in the church who had become Christians in recent years and were quite open in sharing their faith, so when the offer of a team came through the routine baptism follow-up letter she had no hesitation in saying yes. Her husband had no interest whatsoever, so it would obviously be easier for her to do the course during the day when some of the children were at school. Sylvia (the leader), Kath (one of the women June had mentioned she knew) and Yvonne made up the team.

The week before we were due to start, I was suddenly

approached by Carol, who had heard about the course through the women at the Wednesday afternoon 'Open Doors'. This presented me with a dilemma. In normal circumstances I would have arranged a separate team for Carol, especially as she and June did not know each other, but we were so stretched for team members that, after consulting with Sylvia, we decided that we had no choice and would do the course with them together. It certainly made the team's task more difficult, and at one stage we wondered whether we had made a wise decision. However, both women made a commitment to Christ, although June has gone no further so far. Carol, on the other hand, has gone from strength to strength. She was confirmed in May 1988 and is wholehearted in her commitment.

As these examples show, each situation will present a different set of problems and opportunities. On a few occasions our teams have not been able to complete the course, but they form a minute percentage of the total.

CHAPTER FIFTEEN

OUTREACH UNLIMITED

THREE YEARS AGO the parish acquired a photo-copier to fill up some more of the space in my study/office. Its usefulness is such that I find it hard to believe how we ever managed without one. In a nutshell that is rather how I feel about the outreach scheme which has become known as 'Good News Down the Street'. It is such an integral part of parish life that I would find it hard to function without it. Not that parish evangelism cannot be effective without it—there are many imaginative evangelistic initiatives being undertaken around the country—but because its simplicity and versatility make it an invaluable evangelistic tool. It works in so many and varied situations that I really do wonder how I would cope if it wasn't available.

Versatility is perhaps its greatest virtue. It can be tailored to meet the needs of each situation. You can cater for the individual requirements of people in a way that more set forms of evangelism do not easily allow. It is really only an extension of the most basic and effective form of evangelism there is: that of one person sharing with another the good news of Jesus Christ. Wilson Carlisle, the founder of the Church Army once declared: 'I have got the biggest job I have ever tackled in my life. I am trying to open the mouths of the people in the pews.'[1] The scheme encourages even the shyest church members to open their mouths and tell what God has done for them.

All the resources for effective evangelism are already

present in our churches in the lives of our members. Somehow they need to be released from the prison of silence and given confidence to speak, for when they do, people will listen. Evangelism needs to be taken out of the hands of the ministers, the 'professionals', and given back to the people— all the people. Not only will the Christian church then begin to grow again in this country, but the level of commitment and the grasp of Christian truth in our congregations will increase dramatically.

As Roland Allen observed from his experience in China, any attempt to share the faith with another person has a profound effect on the witness:

> The expression of his experience intensifies it; it renews it; it enlightens it. In speaking of it he goes through it again; in setting it before another he sets it before himself in a new light. He gets a deeper sense of its reality and power and meaning. In speaking of it he pledges himself to the conduct and life it involves. He proclaims himself bound by it, and every time that his speech produces an effect upon another, that effect reacts upon himself, making his hold upon his truth surer and stronger.
>
> But this is only if his speech is voluntary and spontaneous. If he is a paid agent, both speaker and hearer are affected by that fact. The speaker knows, and knows that the other knows, that he is employed by a mission to speak. He is not delivering his own message because he cannot help it. He is not speaking of Christ because Christ alone impels him . . .[2]

The professional must always labour under that disadvantage, which is not to say the Church should not have 'professionals', but that they need to know their place and their limitations. As David Edwards so pungently expressed it:

> Christianity has spent much of its history under the severe control of professional priests and preachers. In practical terms it has looked as if the first duty of Christians was to obey and finance the clergy set over them. We need not deny that some full-time officers have been necessary in the Church—and have been its devoted servants. But we recall that the historical Jesus was very much a layman, with a layman's sense of priorities. He did not live in order to found a society for the support of clergymen.[3]

In the field of evangelism lay people have to be the front-line troops; yet how much of their time and energy is taken up with raising money to keep buildings and clergy in action! It must seem to many lay people that there is something wrong with churches' priorities when church maintenance stands in the way of mission. How much better to be engaged in a faith-sharing exercise for six weeks in the home of interested enquirers after truth than to be sitting on a committee organising a fund-raising event to keep the church in business!

The effect of such activity, as Roland Allen affirmed, is to deepen people's faith and commitment. The outreach course, taking place as it does in the relaxed atmosphere of a home, induces hitherto dumb saints to bear witness to their Lord, and that new-found confidence in sharing their faith begins to spill over into everyday situations. One quiet, shy lady, whom I had persuaded to go out on a team, recounted to me one day that, to her own astonishment, she had found herself talking quietly, shyly, but quite naturally about her faith to a stranger on the bus. 'I quite forgot where I was,' she confessed. 'I've got so used to sharing my faith on the team that I didn't remember to get embarrassed!'

As more and more people get the opportunity to go out on teams the new-found confidence that results begins to affect other areas of church life. It raises the level of expectation, and also makes people more aware of the faults, failings and shortcomings of the church. The presence of new Christians, in a steady and continuous stream, is a great lift to the spirit, but it also makes you more conscious of the pitfalls awaiting the innocent newcomer.

The combination of these two factors makes the outreach scheme a powerful tool for change. After all, why *should* a group of Christians meeting for their own enjoyment be expected to change hallowed traditions, time-honoured patterns of worship, familiar hymns that have been sung for centuries, language that is rich and resonant with religious allusions? Does it really matter whether the language of worship is couched in seventeenth-century English, or in Latin, come to that, if all the worshippers have been nurtured in that tradition and understand it? Of course it

doesn't! To change the style and language of worship simply
to bring it up-to-date would make no sense at all. But when
the style and language of worship is so far removed from
everyday use that only those nurtured within the tradition
can participate meaningfully, they will automatically
exclude all but the most persistent outsider.

The influx of complete outsiders joining a hitherto static or
declining congregation can or should be a catalyst for
change. Yet how reluctant church people are to give up their
favourite version of the Bible, or the antiquated hymnbooks,
and use language non-church people can understand; how
reluctant to move to styles of worship that suit the prevailing
culture from which new converts come! So much of our
worship shouts: 'You are not welcome here!' People do not
expect church worship to reflect exactly where they are, but
they do have to be able to relate sufficiently to what is going
on to feel that they belong and will benefit from coming! We
cannot really embark seriously on evangelism unless we are
ready to make the self-sacrifice required of us, not only in
terms of time and energy expended in the evangelistic task,
but also in terms of the way we order our Christian community.

The extent to which the outreach scheme is used as a tool
for change and growth will obviously vary from place to
place. How it is implemented will depend on the vision,
initiative, vigour and perseverance of the church leadership.
It is obviously easier to implement in a small church than a
large one where the minister(s) and key lay people are so
busy keeping all the existing activities running efficiently
that they have neither time nor energy to devote to a radical
programme of restructuring. To motivate and mobilise a
large congregation for continuous evangelism of the sort I
have been describing would be an enormous task. In larger
churches, I suspect, the scheme is unlikely ever to be used
other than as one evangelistic tool among others, operating
well, but never influencing the overall strategy of the church.

I have no doubt in my own mind that it has its greatest
potential in the smaller church, where it can be the means of
renewing the life and vision of the congregation, releasing its

members, and making evangelism central to its purpose. If it becomes the foundation for the ongoing evangelistic strategy of the church, its full potential is realised as more and more lay people get involved. However, this will only happen where the leadership has the vision to set long-term goals and give the scheme top priority for at least three years. Of course, it is demanding on the minister's time and energy in those initial years, but the benefits that spring from making it the hub around which the rest of the church's life rolls are enormous. Charlie, who had experienced it in Chase Terrace, and then went as a curate to Wolverhampton, saw that clearly:

> 'Good News Down the Street' works best when the whole church catches the vision together. Excitement concerning the possibilities, prayer, available contacts—all will grow when the vision is shared by all. My experience is that the more the method is explained, shared and widely used among church members, the sharper is its evangelistic edge.

It may not always be easy at first to persuade the congregation to give it that sort of priority, but if the leadership shares that vision and works towards that end, using every opportunity that arises to send out teams, growing a new congregation alongside the old—the effect will be the same. The steady influx of new Christians will imperceptibly alter the attitudes of long-standing members and make them more ready to accept the importance and value of what is taking place. Constant mention of the course in church notices and publicity; publicly introducing in Sunday services those who become Christians through the course; the new Christians' own informal personal testimony to its value to them—all help to build a climate of confidence which will ease the way for it to become a permanent and central part of the church's life. It will also become known to the wider community, those with whom church members have contact. The friends, relatives and neighbours of new converts will certainly get to hear of it. Over a period of time many people will register its existence, be aware of its impact and be more open to the possibility of inviting a team into their own home.

When the local church is involved in an ongoing scheme of

evangelism such as this it gives the good news of Jesus a higher profile. Because it is the local initiative of local people, it is perceived as more credible and more relevant by the local community. Its results are its best advertisement, as the slimming industry realises:

> People tried the F-Plan, found they could keep to it, discovered they were losing weight more easily and speedily than ever before, and triumphantly told their friends: 'It works!' And then the news spread . . . The real reason for the F-Plan sensation is summed up in those two words: 'It works.'[4]

The good news we declare is, we believe, of far greater importance than any scheme for losing weight; but that will only become apparent as more and more people triumphantly (or just quietly!) tell their friends: 'It works!'. If 'Good News Down the Street' has helped more people just to do that it has served its purpose.

NOTES

1 *Towards the Conversion of England* (London: 1945), p53.
2 Roland Allen, *The Spontaneous Expansion of the Church* (Eerdmans: Grand Rapids, Michigan, 1962), p11.
3 David Edwards, *Jesus for the Modern Man* (Collins/Fontana: London, 1975), p134.
4 Preface to Audrey Eyton's *The Fibre Plan Diet Book* (Penguin: London, 1982).

The Growth Book

by Dr Roy Pointer

Turn theory into reality: your church *can* grow!

Are you eager for growth in your church, but frustrated by lack of practical knowledge? THE GROWTH BOOK, which is designed for group study, will guide you through the basic principles of Church Growth and show you how to apply them to your local situation. The eight sessions help you to:
— Learn how churches can grow
— Discover how your own church is growing or declining
— Identify the key signs of growth
— Use church surveys properly
— Recognise your spiritual gifts
— Plan effective outreach
— Evaluate your church's meetings
— Set realistic goals for the growth of your church
To help your group's creative thinking, each session contains Bible studies, leader's notes, discussion questions and testing exercises, with guidance for further study.

This book can help *your* church to grow.

MARC
Monarch Publications